D1563723

WITHDRAWN

CHARLES DICKENS' CHILDHOOD

Charles Dickens' Childhood

Michael Allen

St. Martin's Press   New York

First published in the United States of America in 1988

Printed in Hong Kong

ISBN 0–312–01275–6

Library of Congress Cataloging-in-Publication Data
Allen, Michael, 1945–
Charles Dickens' childhood/by Michael Allen.
p.   cm.
Bibliography: p. 134.
Includes index.
ISBN 0–312–01275–6: $30.00 (est.)
1. Dickens, Charles, 1812–1870—Biography—Youth.   2. Novelists,
English—19th century—Biography.   I. Title.
PR4582.A44   1988
823'.8—dc19
[B]
                                                    87–20302
                                                         CIP

This book is for Barbara Allen

Contents

Acknowledgements

Thanks are due to Victor Neuburg for his early encouragement to carry out research work; to David Parker, Curator of Dickens House, for his constant assistance; and to my wife Barbara for her patience. Acknowledgements are also due to the following organisations for permission to reproduce material held in their collections: The British Library Reference Division, The British Library Newspaper Library, Hampshire County Library Portsmouth, Portsmouth City Records Office, City of Westminster Libraries Archives Department, The Public Record Office, London Borough of Southwark Public Libraries, Greater London Record Office (Maps and Prints), Royal Commission on the Historical Monuments of England, London Borough of Camden Libraries and Arts Department, Portsmouth City Museums, Barbara Allen, The Dickens House Museum.

List of Plates

Chronological List

DICKENS' CHILDHOOD HOMES

1.	Mile End Terrace, Portsmouth	7 Feb 1812–24 Jun 1812
2.	16 Hawke Street, Portsmouth	25 Jun 1812–25 Dec 1813
3.	39 Wish Street, Southsea	26 Dec 1813–25 Dec 1814
4.	10 Norfolk Street, St Marylebone	26 Dec 1814–25 Dec 1816
5.	High Street, Blue Town, Sheerness	26 Dec 1816–4 Apr 1817
6.	Ordnance Terrace, Chatham	5 April 1817–4 Apr 1821
7.	St Mary's Place, The Brook, Chatham	5 Apr 1821–24 Jun 1822
8.	Giles' School, Best Street, Chatham	25 Jun 1822–Sept 1822
9.	16 Bayham Street, Camden Town	Sept 1822–25 Dec 1823
10.	4 Gower Street North, St Pancras	26 Dec 1823–4 Apr 1824
11.	37 Little College Street, Camden Town	5 Apr 1824–1 May 1824
12.	1 Lant Street, Borough	2 May 1824–27 May 1824
13.	37 Little College Street, Camden Town	28 May 1824–29 Sep 1824
14.	Hampstead	30 Sep 1824–25 Dec 1824
15.	29 Johnson Street, Somers Town	26 Dec 1824–1827

Introduction

The aim of this book has been to approach the childhood of Charles Dickens with a fresh eye: certainly to examine the work of past biographers, but also to question their facts and opinions; to test their accuracy by going back to original sources; and to seek out new sources and new information.

There is a long history of enquiry into Dickens' early life, that history having had a ragged beginning, as documented by Engel.[1] The details of his childhood did not come quickly to the attention of the public, and when they did come they were not always accurate. Dickens himself provided the very earliest résumé, in a letter written in 1838, when he gave some brief information for publication in Germany:

> I was born at Portsmouth, an English Seaport town principally remarkable for mud, Jews, and Sailors, on the 7th. of February 1812. My father holding in those days a situation under Government in the Navy Pay Office, which called him in the discharge of his duty to different places, I came to London, a child of two years old, left it again at six, and then left it again for another Sea Port town – Chatham – where I remained some six or seven years, and then came back to London with my parents and half a dozen brothers and sisters, whereof I was second in seniority.
>
> I had begun an irregular rambling education under a clergyman at Chatham, and I finished it at a good school in London – tolerably early, for my father was not a rich man, and I had to begin the world.[2]

He ended the letter 'I have said more about myself in this one note than I should venture to say elsewhere in twenty years'. Nor did he say more: further details of his childhood were kept conspiratorially quiet until after Dickens' death, so that even his children were unaware of the hardships he had suffered during part of his early life. The silence was broken in 1872, with the publication of Forster's biography of Dickens; but invaluable though that book was – and is – it still did not provide either a full or an accurate account of Dickens' early life. Attempts have been

1

made ever since to fill the gaps. Forster's account depended very heavily on information from Dickens himself, to which he added some reminiscences from his subject's schoolfriends, and these personal accounts were subsequently expanded by other authors through articles and letters published in various periodicals.

Throughout the thirty years following Dickens' death many items of a topographical nature were also published, concentrating primarily on descriptions of the locations in which Dickens' novels were set, with occasional added brief descriptions of some of the houses in which he lived. One account – that of Robert Langton – stands out above the others. By seeking out those people still living who remembered the Dickens family, and consulting various official records, he was able to add considerably to Forster's account of Dickens' childhood: he was the first person, for example, to mention Dickens' home at Ordnance Terrace, Chatham. Also worthy of note during this period is the work of F. G. Kitton, who similarly sought out contemporaries of Dickens and tried to fix more accurately the dates of the family's movements.

During the first half of the twentieth century little information was added to what was already known of the early life of Dickens, though Gladys Storey did throw forward some debatable points: debatable since her information came from Dickens' elderly daughter Kate, and Dickens is reported to have told his children very little of his childhood. The most outstanding publication since 1950 has been Edgar Johnson's biography, which presents a formidable challenge to any author seeking to replace it. However, its value as the best authority on Dickens' early life is doubtful: it weaves previously available information into an attractive narrative, but presents little new information.

The prize for post-war research work on Dickens' early life must go to W. J. Carlton, who presented a number of impressive articles through the pages of *The Dickensian*. That periodical also published two extremely well-researched articles by Angus Easson, both throwing much-needed light on the affairs of John Dickens. It is a great pity that the work of Carlton and Easson was not taken into account by Johnson when he prepared a new edition of his work. Gaps and mistakes appearing in the first edition (1953) are repeated in the new edition (1977). Neither does a new biography by N. and J. Mackenzie (1979) take advantage of the material available, or produce fresh information of its own.

In writing this book I have concentrated on seeking out rarely-used or unused details, and have sought to weld that information with the most valuable material from the past, thus producing new insights into the early life of Dickens. The results are intended to correct and supersede past biographers wherever possible. Many of the new details sought have centred on the homes of the Dickens family and the dates of their movements between homes. The following set of questions provided a skeletal frame, to which the flesh was gradually added: (1) What are the locations of the precise buildings that were homes of Charles Dickens and his family? (2) What information can be gathered on those buildings? (3) In what sort of communities were the buildings located? (4) What were the exact dates of occupation by the Dickens family? (5) What was the structure of the Dickens family and household, and what details of their lives can be gathered? (6) What fresh assessments can be made from the information gathered?

To answer the first question a working list of known homes was constructed from biographies of Dickens, care being taken to examine very early works, as well as the most recent and most prominent. The addresses listed were then checked against the appropriate rate books, and it should be noted here what information rate books do and do not give. Rates were levied for a number of reasons: for example, to provide assistance to the poor, to maintain a jail, to provide for the paving, lighting and watering of the streets. They may have been levied at regular intervals – most often, at this period, every six months – or on isolated occasions. Rate books usually indicate the date that a rate was levied and the period it was intended to cover, always between Quarter Days, which fell on or about 25 March (Lady Day), 24 June (Midsummer Day), 29 September (Michaelmas Day) and 25 December (Christmas Day). They show the person responsible for the rate (usually the occupant), the ratable value of the property (intended to be the sum for which the property could be rented) and the rate due. Additional information is sometimes given, such as the non-payment of rates and subsequent summons, the departure or arrival of occupants, or the ownership of the property. Exact addresses are not necessarily given: it should be borne in mind that the first quarter of the nineteenth century was a time of rapid housing expansion, a time when the need for exact addresses was only just being recognised. Darlington[3] points out that street numbering did not take place in most provincial towns until about 1825–50.

Information given in the rate books at Portsmouth reflects well this state of development: the house now known to be the birthplace of Charles Dickens is listed in the rate books only as a property somewhere in the area known as New Town; at Hawke Street, however, the street is clearly named and each house numbered; at Wish Street, where new houses were being built every year, the name is given, but only some of the houses are numbered, and examination of subsequent rate books shows that the houses changed numbers erratically before settling down to a regular pattern. The situation was different in Chatham: there the town was divided into four boroughs, and the rate books merely list all ratepayers within each borough, indicating neither house number nor name of street. It can be seen, then, that information from the rate books had to be used in conjunction with details from elsewhere.

These details came from a variety of sources. For example, examination of Portsmouth local newspapers for 1812 uncovered a remarkable advertisement, showing that a house in Mile End Terrace, recently occupied by Mr John Dickens, is available for sale, with further particulars to be had from Mr William Pearce, thus fixing not only an address more precise than that given in the rate books, but also the owner of the property. Equally remarkable is the survival of the rent book kept by that owner, listing the persons from whom he collected rent, the amount collected and the period that the rent covered. Addresses are not given in this rent book, but the precise house occupied by John Dickens was described in a letter from William Pearce's son, written in 1883.

Maps, too, proved to be of enormous importance for locating houses. A wide variety were examined, dating from the beginning of the nineteenth century up to the current day. Two sets of maps, both showing individual houses, were of exceptional importance: the first edition Ordnance Survey 50":1 mile (c. 1860–80) and a collection of maps held by the Street Numbering Department of the Greater London Council.

Biographies of Dickens and topographical books were also helpful, these providing in some instances the only real evidence of an address (Kitton's evidence for Hawke Street in Portsmouth; Forster's mention of Norfolk Street in London). Of additional use were photographs, many of them taken at the beginning of this century, and street directories, a fine collection of which is held at the Guildhall Library in the City of London.

Using a combination of these sources it has been possible to locate the precise sites of all but two of the buildings in which Charles Dickens lived during the period covered. The two exceptions are an address in Hampstead and another in Sheerness, the latter ignored by biographers for more than a hundred years. All those sites located have been clearly presented in this book on specially-drawn maps. Findings of particular interest at this level are the address and location of the house in Wish Street, Southsea, together with the incidental connection of that address with a passage in the book by Dolby; the approximate location of a house at Sheerness; the address and location of Charles Dickens' lodgings at Lant Street in London; and the location of the houses at Gower Street North and Little College Street.

The approach to the second question – What information about those buildings can be gathered? – involved gathering information on the living accommodation of the Dickens family, the style of the houses in which they lived and the terms of their occupation. The information gathered went towards an assessment of their way of life, their social standing and their financial situation.

The rate books were again of use here, giving an indication of the rent John Dickens paid; or, by not listing him, indicating that he was a lodger rather than a tenant. The rate books show that with one exception John Dickens was consistent in the value of the property he rented, ranging narrowly between £16 and £22 a year; other accommodation in the streets where he lived was rated as low as £4 and as high as £50. The one exception, Gower Street North, was indeed rated at £50 and would seem to have been taken on the suggestion of Mrs Dickens. Perhaps it is not surprising to note that John Dickens moved from his most expensive accommodation to his cheapest – the Marshalsea Prison! It is worth bearing in mind at this point the possible discrepancies between the rated value and the rented value, though the two should have been equivalents. It is known, for example, from William Pearce's rent book that John Dickens paid an annual rent of £35, yet that same property was rated at only £18. The questions are then raised: was the rating system completely out of touch with reality, or were the rating officers being misled, or was John Dickens being overcharged for that particular rent?

An advertisement in the Portsmouth newspapers made it clear that the house at Mile End Terrace would have been intended for a family fitting the description of 'genteel'; and, because there was such a small difference in rated value between the houses that he rented, this would almost certainly have applied to the others too. It is interesting to note the number of new, or almost new, houses that John Dickens moved into: Mile End Terrace, Wish Street, Ordnance Terrace, Bayham Street and Gower Street North; even Johnson Street was, by today's standards, comparatively new.

The sizes and styles of the buildings have been judged from large-scale maps and photographs, most of the photographs being held in the Tyrrel Collection at the Dickens House Museum in London. None of the houses were particularly large, and though to modern taste they may appear to have been overcrowded, this would have been quite acceptable to the usually large nineteenth-century family. Where possible the internal layout of the house has been described, either from personal observation, as at Mile End Terrace, or from information given in past biographical and topographical works: of outstanding interest here was the book by Langstaff on Johnson Street.

Of incidental interest at this stage was the manner in which people set about finding accommodation in the first quarter of the nineteenth century: the local newspapers were obviously of some value in the process and not to be ignored. And it is clear that William Pearce considered the name of John Dickens as an ex-tenant to be something of an asset in the selling of his house. Some of the newspaper advertisements in this book are reproduced for the first time in book form.

Moving on to the third question – In what sort of communities were the buildings located? – information was sought, wherever possible, from sources other than past studies on Dickens, so that fresh insights could be presented. At both Portsmouth and Chatham contemporary local newspapers were scanned and the findings combined with more recent studies. The availability of newspapers for this research certainly proved valuable and yielded much information; yet, since the volume of newspaper material is so great, particularly in London, and the searching is so time-consuming and wearisome, there is much that has not been covered. It follows that further information of intrinsic value must still lie hidden.

For Portsmouth and Chatham information on the way of life in the towns at that time was sought from books and documents in the public library local history collections, the archive collections and the museums. Maps, illustrations and books were scanned, and a combination of these have been used to represent the atmosphere of the towns. Of particular interest at Chatham were first the books by Hobbes and Presnail, and second the writings of Dickens himself, which give a unique description of life at Ordnance Terrace.

In London the newspapers were more numerous, and also more concerned with national and international news, and so were not closely examined. Here the most valuable document was Dickens' autobiographical sequence, given by Forster. It has been supplemented, however, by information taken from books held at public library local history collections, an excellent description of Bayham Street from a contemporary of Dickens, and a number of illustrations from both local and national libraries. The illustration of the house in Lant Street is worth particular attention.

The fourth question was: What were the exact dates of occupation by the Dickens family? The approach here was first to arrange a list of possible dates at each address by reference to past biographies and then, by gathering as many documented dates as possible, to adjust the structure as work progressed. Admiralty records, held at the Public Record Office in London, provided details of John Dickens' movements between London and the outports, Church records placed him in particular places at particular times and rate books fixed him to certain houses. Throughout the research for this book the importance of Quarter Days became increasingly clear when fixing dates of removal. This is when rents were due to be paid (as indicated in William Pearce's rent book) and when, for one reason or another, tenants moved on. Dickens himself wrote of Lant Street: 'The population is migratory, usually disappearing on the verge of quarter-day, and generally by night.'[4]

A number of important details have arisen from the dates fixed by my research. It has been shown that at Portsmouth Dickens lived in Wish Street for a year – a substantial period – and that he was brought to London around 1 January 1815. The Dickens family's stay in London has been fixed quite firmly at two years exactly from that date and it has been shown that, following a period of five years in Chatham, the Dickens family returned to

London in June 1822, earlier than biographers have previously reported (though Charles did not travel with them at that time).

But the most important point to be recognised in this area of the book is that Charles Dickens spent much longer than has been presumed at Warren's Blacking. The length of this period is crucial to the understanding of his reaction to it – far-reaching as the effect of this was on his life and on the books he wrote – and accounts of this period must now be reconsidered in the light of the information presented here.

For the fifth question – What was the structure of the Dickens family and household, and what details of their lives can be gathered? – the method was first to examine the major biographies of Dickens, together with his own writings and speeches, and second to search such sources as *The Dickensian*, scrapbooks of periodical articles and Admiralty records. The wealth of material held at the Dickens House Museum in London was particularly valuable at this point. So too was that at the Public Record Office in London, where details were found of the salary of John Dickens, letters relating to his retirement and descriptions of his work as a pay clerk. Illustrations of John and Elizabeth Dickens have been included, as well as another, held at Dickens House Museum, claimed to be of Charles as a boy but not, it is believed, previously published in book form.

In making fresh assessments of Dickens' early life – the last of the questions asked – this book necessarily deals not only with the childhood of Charles Dickens, but also with the life and career of his father (within the period covered), and develops a more sympathetic view of him than has generally been the case with past biographers. It recognises the degree of success he achieved at the Navy Pay Office, the optimistic manner in which he sought to rise from a humble background and the serious setbacks he suffered. The flaws in his character, which are given much greater prominence subsequent to the period covered here, should be seen in the light of Dickens' own comment on his father, written to Forster in 1865: 'my poor father, whom I regard as a better man the longer I live'.[5] Earlier, in his autobiographical fragment, he had written: 'I know my father to be as kindhearted and generous a man as ever lived in the world. Everything I can remember of his conduct to his wife, or children, or friends, in sickness or affliction, is beyond all praise. By me, as a sick child, he has watched night and day, unweariedly and patiently, many nights and days. He never undertook any business, charge or trust, that he did not zealously, conscientiously, punctually, honourably discharge. His industry has always been untiring.'[6]

Throughout the writing of this book the recognition of John Dickens' influence on his son has become increasingly pronounced. In his literary career – and the social life which accompanied it – Charles Dickens certainly aimed high. It would appear that he was emulating his father's own aim of achieving a richer life, in every sense of the phrase, the basic difference between the two being that John Dickens had only a belief in optimism, energy and good fortune upon which to build his better life, while his son had a phenomenal talent. A good example of this trait in their two characters is manifested by John Dickens' encouragement to the young Charles that he might one day own Gads Hill Place if he worked hard, and Charles' later achievement of that ownership. I see paralleled, also, the despondency of Charles in his own prison of Warren's Blacking, and the despondency of his father on entering the real Marshalsea Prison. In both cases high hopes were bitterly dashed to the ground.

The basic optimism, the recognition that the highest aims in life were possible to achieve – which were so large a part of Charles Dickens' character and were instilled by his father – and the confidence and awareness of a genteel background built up in Chatham must be fully appreciated to recognise the gross disappointment, the waste and boredom of life at Bayham Street, and then the shattering shame of his father's imprisonment and the misery of his own employment in a boot-blacking factory. The time at Chatham proved to be the most secure period in Dickens' childhood. At Chatham the genteel way of life in an otherwise violent and bawdy town formed Charles' view of his family's position in the community and his own expectations from life: here John Dickens enjoyed his best ever income, the family employed two servants and Charles thrived on success and encouragement at school, visits to the theatre, books to read, parties to go to, friends to play with. No doubt John Dickens' plans for his eldest son were expansive, and known to be so: possibly the ownership of Gads Hill Place, possibly a place at university.

It was the sharp contrast, the depth of the fall, that proved so bitter – and the length of the period. Yet though his father had brought him such misery, so too had he provided him with the sort of character that would combat and overcome such setbacks: optimism and belief in self provided a determination that eventually turned his setbacks into advantages, and a sort of inoculating protection against further similar rebuttals.

This book notes John Dickens' own early preoccupation with areas that were later to become passionate pursuits of his son. John Dickens, for example, made use of his ability to write, taking up journalism as a second career; and Charles too was encouraged to contribute 'penny-a-line items' to the newspapers, developing this small beginning into a lifelong passion for journalism. It can be seen, too, that Charles was encouraged to take an interest in the theatre and in performing – anything from Shakespeare to comic singing. Nor was the family's encouragement restricted to Charles: witness the enormous help given to his sister Fanny to develop as a musician. In both cases the encouragement was well placed.

The book draws attention to the unsettled nature of the Dickens household, involving for Charles fourteen moves in as many years. It is worth considering the effect this may have had on his later life, relating it in particular to the restlessness of his nature and his constant need to travel, whether abroad to Switzerland, France, Italy or America, or at home to Richmond, Broadstairs, Cornwall or the Isle of Wight. He seemed unable to settle for any length of time in one place, even though he owned only three permanent homes between 1839 and 1870. This reflects both a need for the settled home that he never had as a child, and a need to be continually on the move. The restlessness of his own childhood may also have been reflected in the unsettled home lives of many of his characters during their childhood and/or youth: Oliver Twist, Little Nell, Pip and David Copperfield, for example.

This then has been the approach to the writing of the book. Throughout the long history of enquiry into the life of Charles Dickens there has been a gradual growth in the body of known information, much of the information superseding that which has gone before. This book has sought to continue that process of evolution.

1

Portsmouth

ELIZABETH AND WILLIAM DICKENS

I find it odd that a certain man's life had ultimately a profound and far-reaching effect on the world, yet that man knew nothing of it. Nobody ever intended to leave an account of the life of William Dickens, let alone the man himself, yet diligent researchers have tracked down his name recorded on at least three different documents. First there is a marriage register showing that he wed Elizabeth Ball at St George's, Hanover Square, London, on 22 November 1781.[1] Second there are entries in the accounts books of the Crewe family – who had property at 18 Lower Grosvenor Street, London, Crewe Hall in Cheshire, and Madeley Manor in Staffordshire – showing that William Dickens was their butler and responsible for paying staff and maintaining accounts.[2] Third there is a record of his burial in one of the grounds of St George's, on 10 October 1785.[3] It is also known that he had one son, born in 1783, whom he named after himself, and another, born sometime between April 1785 and March 1786, whom he or his wife called John.[4] Examination of these dates shows clearly that this second son may well have been born after the death of his father.

Though little enough is known of this particular butler, it is known that butlers in general were a superior class of people, exerting great authority over other servants, commanding respect from those they served and occupying positions of trust. On the whole it took many years to attain such a position, and one authority has estimated that William Dickens was aged about 66 when he died.[5] One other important fact remains: on his death he left to his wife the handsome sum of £450, which was invested in 3% Consols at the Bank of England.

This investment may or may not have been some small consolation to Elizabeth Dickens for the awkward predicament in which she was left: a widowed servant with one two-year-old child and another on the way or just born. She had been a servant before her marriage, with Lady Blandford of Grosvenor Square, and is known to have been housekeeper to the Crewe family by 1798, so presumably she took up service with her husband's employers on her marriage. It says much for her own qualities as a servant, or for the kindness of the Crewe family, that her position was retained after the death of William Dickens. After all, the employment of a servant with two babies must have had its disadvantages. Nevertheless Elizabeth Dickens was clearly much valued by her employers, attaining the important position of housekeeper, a position that usually carried with it responsibility for the running of certain aspects of the household, including the hiring, firing and control of the other female servants. She was later remembered with great affection by the children of the Crewe family:

> Lady Houghton used to tell that when she was a child the greatest treat that could be given to her brother and herself and sister was an afternoon in the housekeeper's room at Crewe, for Mrs. Dickens was an inimitable story-teller, and she loved to have the children around her, and to beguile them, not only with fairy tales, but with reminiscences of her own, and stories from the pages of history.[6]

As to the upbringing of her two sons, nothing is known. Yet, living in the household of a wealthy family, they were clearly well cared for, secure and fully aware of a superior style of life. As far as is known, John Dickens lived with his mother – and the Crewe family – until the age of nineteen. This does seem rather late for the son of a servant to be first put to work, and it is therefore probable that other tasks would have been found for him, even if these were only as an additional servant to the Crewe family.

However that may be, it is clearly recorded in Admiralty records that John Dickens was appointed as an 'extra clerk' in the office of the Treasurer of His Majesty's Navy on 5 April 1805,[7] following the expansion of that office by George Canning, the Treasurer of the Navy. The necessity for increasing the number of clerks in the Navy Pay Office by eight is given in letters from Canning to the Lords Commissioners of the Admiralty, dated 31 December 1804 and 8 February 1805.[8] It has been suggested by past biographers that John Dickens had been pushed forward by Lord Crewe, a friend of George Canning. Be that as it may, he found himself attending the very grand Admiralty offices at Somerset House in London's Strand, together with the seven other new clerks,[9] one of whom was Thomas Barrow, who struck up a particular friendship with John Dickens, frequently taking him home.

It is recorded in still-available Admiralty records that these newcomers were in receipt of five shillings for each day of attendance at their workplace, giving them an annual salary of just over £78. For John Dickens this financial reward continued over nearly two years, until 23 January 1807, when he was appointed to the permanent position of '15th assistant clerk for the general business of the Pay Branch'.[10] For this he earned a slightly lower basic salary of £70 per annum but received in addition two shillings for each day of attendance – about £30 a year. Twice during 1807 he moved up the Navy Pay Office hierarchical ladder, in Midsummer to 14th assistant clerk and at Christmas to 13th assistant clerk.[11] These changes of position did not entitle him to more money: that came only with long service; but from 7 November 1807[12] he was moved from Somerset House to one of the navy ports, and for this his income rose, for attendance only, from two shillings to five shillings per day, or to about £91 per annum.

It is not absolutely certain to which port John Dickens was sent at this time, although it is known that at one point during his period at Somerset House he was sent down to Portsmouth Docks on an errand, carrying a private despatch to the Chief Clerk of the Pay Yard and accompanying back to London the wife of the Paymaster of the Forces, who was, from 1806 to 1807, the dramatist Sheridan.[13] Small connections between the Dickens family and the theatre are worth plotting throughout this book, and this first connection should be duly noted: could the conversation on that journey have revolved primarily around the theatrical achievements of Sheridan, and could a spark have been lit, or fanned, in John Dickens that was later to have far-reaching effects on his famous son? It is also interesting to note here that Sheridan's *School for Scandal* was dedicated to Lady Crewe.

The errand may well have given the Chief Clerk at Portsmouth an opportunity to assess John Dickens as a possible member of his staff, and it seems likely that John Dickens became part of the Pay Office there from the end of 1807; he was certainly there the following year, when a letter dated 24 August 1808 was sent to their employers by five Portsmouth clerks, including John Dickens.[14]

The following tables, taken from Admiralty records, show first John Dickens' salary scale, which came into operation on 3 August 1808, and second his annual income throughout his career with the Navy Pay Office.[15]

Salary scale

1st–3rd years	£101	6s
4th–5th	£110	0s
6th–7th	£120	0s
8th–10th	£140	0s
11th–15th	£200	0s
16th–25th	£350	0s
26 years plus	£500	0s

Income

1805	£56	15s	
1806	£78	5s	
1807	£109	16s	1d
1808	£196	7s	7d
1809	£201	5s	
1810	£208	15s	
1811	£211	5s	
1812	£225	18s	11d
1813	£231	5s	
1814	£231	5s	
1815	£191	2s	
1816	£200	0s	
1817	£289	15s	
1818	£291	5s	
1819	£291	5s	
1820	£403	10s	
1821	£441	0s	
1822	£441	0s	
1823	£350	0s	
1824	£350	0s	
1825	£230	0s	
1826–1851	£145	16s	8d

PORTSMOUTH, 1808–14

Portsmouth, during the seven years that John Dickens lived there and during the first three years of Charles Dickens' life, was a busy, growing town. As a major naval establishment it was in the forefront of the war against Napoleon and later against America. The local newspapers of this period are full of reports of ships coming and going, of the presence in the town of important naval personnel, and of news of battles won and lost. There was an excitement about the town. The newspapers give many reports, too, concerning prisoners of war held at Portsmouth: rebellions on board the hulk ships, attempted escapes, successful escapes and subsequent pursuits, and occasionally news of a prisoner of war being granted his freedom, as on one occasion for saving a seaman from drowning.

The maintenance of ships in the harbour, their provision and the payment of officers, sailors and artificers created much employment, including of course that of John Dickens. His job was not an easy one. Details of part of his work, the paying of artificers, is given in a letter sent from pay clerks at Portsmouth:[16] between one and two o'clock each Saturday the pay lists would be delivered to the clerks and payment would begin immediately. The naval yard was split into gangs of workers, and payment would be made to the leader of each gang. These leaders would provide a list of the men in their gang and the amount payable to them. This would be checked by the pay clerks against their own lists, and if the two corresponded payment would be made. The payments would be in quantities of notes, silver and copper sufficient to distribute among the gang, and up to £6600 would be handed out each week. Because of the amounts involved, the numbers of workers employed and, in winter, the fact that the handouts were made by candlelight, overpayment was often made. Unfortunately such overpayment was deducted from the pay clerks' salaries, and amounted in 1813, for example, to between ten shillings and £12 13s each week. Understandably a representation was made by the pay clerks at Portsmouth, including John Dickens, to have these overpayments reimbursed. The representation was accepted.

The clerks also had to go out to the ships to pay out the crews, a sometimes hazardous task, as pointed out in another letter from the clerks to their employers; 'from the nature of their duties they are called upon to make constant and large payments on board His Majesty's ships under all the disadvantages of weather and accommodation and consequently incur risks of loss of Property and even personal danger'.[17] There was danger in the streets of Portsmouth, too. The local newspapers give many instances of sailors brawling, of robbery in the streets and of housebreaking. There seems to have been a plethora of road accidents, with many people, particularly children, being crushed by wagon wheels: there was a campaign by one newspaper against wagon drivers driving while sitting on the shafts of their vehicles. The frequency with which they fell off and were crushed by their own wheels seems peculiarly ludicrous, serious though it must have been.

MILE END TERRACE

John Dickens' appointment to Portsmouth could not have proved welcome to him considering that, during his visits to the home of Thomas Barrow back in London, he had fallen in love with his friend's sister, Elizabeth. The father of this brother and sister was Charles Barrow, who held a position of some importance as Chief Conductor of Money at the Navy Office in London. Pursuing courtship over the seventy miles between London and Portsmouth, though difficult, was obviously not beyond the young clerk, aided no doubt by his grandiloquent pen. In June 1809 he travelled back to London to marry Elizabeth Barrow, the ceremony taking place at St Mary-le-Strand, near Somerset House, on the thirteenth of the month.

They then travelled back to Portsmouth, where John Dickens had taken the tenancy of a new house at Mile End Terrace, in an area referred to in the local rate books as New Town, though sometimes known before, and better known afterwards, as Mile End. This house was probably the first to be built in a small terrace of four. Its owner, William Pearce, was an interesting man, judging from the oddments of information about him that can be gathered. In the Portsmouth Street Directory for 1798 William Pearce is listed as a Mercer and Draper, while two other Pearces, Robert and Joseph, were grocer and victualler respectively. He must have done well at his business, since a book listing rents due to him from 1808 onwards indicates ownership of fifteen to twenty houses.[18] John Dickens appears among the tenants, paying his first quarter's rent of £8 15s on 29 June 1809 and continuing through to 24 June 1812. However, John Dickens' name does not appear in the rate books until 25 January 1810; and the rental value is given there as only £18 per annum, half of what he was in fact paying. Further entries appear in the rate books for 5 February 1811 and 22 June 1812. Rents would have been paid in arrears, which means that John Dickens occupied the house from the first week of April 1809. Since Mile End Terrace was situated on the main Portsmouth to London road he had probably seen the house being built, had taken it and had had it furnished and decorated between April and June. It is not possible to say where he lived prior to Mile End Terrace: possibly in lodgings in the Hawke Street area, since this is where, some years later, he took his family after leaving Mile End Terrace.

William Pearce lived in the house next to John Dickens. Built about 1800, and still standing today, it is a large, double-fronted, bay-windowed building, called originally Highland House. Somewhere nearby, perhaps even on the land on which the Dickens home was built, Pearce owned a brewhouse up to 1809; and from 1811 he took over or had built a windmill, situated some 120 feet behind Mile End Terrace, in Mill Lane. This windmill is clearly shown on a contemporary map (see Plate 9) and was of some considerable value, being rated at £40, or £10 more than Highland House itself.

In 1812 Pearce was concerning himself with land enclosure, playing host to a meeting of the proprietors of lands and grounds at another of his properties, the George Inn at nearby Cosham.[19] By 1823–4 he is described in the Street Directory as a grocer, with shops at Queen Street, Broad Street and Half-way Houses. He died on 7 September 1846 at the ripe old age of 84. His daughters lived in the Dickens house until the death of the last of them, Sarah Pearce, in 1903; it was then put out to auction, bought by the Portsmouth Corporation at an enormously inflated price (£1125, compared with the £625 that the house next door fetched at the same auction) and made into the Dickens Birthplace Museum. William Pearce's son, also William, became a solicitor and passed on for posterity the rent book of the house in which Charles Dickens was born. This rent book contains a list of names, the amount of rent due from each person and the period that the rent covers. It does not indicate an address.

The New Town or Mile End area was, as its names suggest, a new development of houses, small in extent, built just one mile from Landport Gate on the main London road. It was in this first quarter of the nineteenth century that development outside the ramparts of old Portsmouth and Portsea first began. Small dwellings for the dockyard workers were built only just outside the fortifications; but the Mile End area was intended more for the equivalent of today's lower-middle-class families. Up to this time the area was completely rural in character, with a few isolated farms and buildings. Behind Mile End Terrace lay open fields looking across to Portsmouth Harbour, just 400 yards away, and out to Whale Island. In addition to the windmill owned by William Pearce, directly behind Mile End Terrace, there were four more situated on the shoreline. The front of the house looked over Cherry Garden Field, which stretched nearly half a mile across to the Kingston Road, where at St Mary's Church Charles Dickens was baptised on 4 March 1812.[20]

The house at Mile End Terrace had been hastily built, with little regard for lasting qualities. It comprised a cellar, which contained a kitchen, coal store and pantry; a ground floor, with a narrow entrance hall which led to the centre of the house, a parlour or withdrawing room – the main family room of the house – overlooking the street and the small front garden, and the dining room at the rear; the first floor, reached by a narrow winding stair which stretched from the cellar to the attic, containing two bedrooms, the front one of which was the birthroom of Charles Dickens; and, at the top of the house, two rather cramped garret rooms off a small square landing. The privy was at the bottom of the garden. There was no running water, this being carried through the streets and bought at a halfpenny a bucket. Oil and candles were used to light the house.

A shadow passed across the Dickens marriage in February 1810 when Elizabeth's father, Charles Barrow, had to flee the country following the discovery by the Admiralty that, through systematic embezzlement, he had defrauded his employers of the sum of £5689 13s 3d. Distressing though this must have been, it seems to have made little difference to the material position of the young couple. Their home must have been comfortable during their first year of marriage. Even a guest could be accommodated in comfort. The arrival of their first child on 28 October 1810 would not have made a lot of difference. She was named Frances Elizabeth,

Frances not being a usual family name, but Elizabeth following her mother, and her grandmother on her father's side; she became known by the family as Fanny. When Charles arrived on the scene eighteen months later, on 7 February 1812, space probably became a little more restricted.

Apparently Elizabeth Dickens told her granddaughter Kate, many years later, that she was dancing at an officers' ball the night before Charles was born.[21] However, a ball that night was neither advertised in the local newspapers, nor reported on. Nevertheless, a ball was held on Monday 3 February, and was indeed reported on the very same page of the newspaper that announced the birth of Charles. The report read: 'On Monday last a grand ball and supper were given by the officers of the Royal Marine mess of this division, at their new Mess Room; which was attended by upwards of 200 persons from this place and the neighbourhood. A very elegant supper was served up at one o'clock, consisting of every delicacy of the season. The room was superbly ornamented with flowers, shrubs, and orange trees, with fruit hanging from the bough. The company were highly entertained and separated at a late hour.' Possibly the mother-to-be attended this ball and the story later became slightly exaggerated. William Pearce the younger later reported: 'I was born on the 22nd February 1814, and have often heard my mother say that Mr. Gardner, the surgeon, and Mrs. Purkis, the monthly nurse (both of whom attended my mother with me and her six other children), attended Mrs. Dickens with her two children, Fanny and Charles'.[22]

The entry into the world of Charles Dickens was proudly announced, through the pages of the Portsmouth newspapers, on 10 February 1812, with the following pronouncement:

BIRTHS – On Friday, at Mile-end Terrace, the Lady of John Dickens, Esq. a son.[23]

Such pride in his new offspring tells us something positive about the extrovert character of John Dickens. Announcements of this kind were not yet common practice for a man of John Dickens' social position. The aspirations of the father shine through this small announcement: note that telling phrase 'the Lady of John Dickens, Esq.'

Evidence suggests that a servant was employed at this time:

Charles later recollected that a nurse watched him from the kitchen window as he trotted about the front garden.[24] This could not have been at Mile End Terrace, since he was too small to walk while there; but if a nurse was employed at a later date then she may well have also been employed at this time, when there were two small babies to look after. The Dickens family certainly employed servants for many years afterwards.

Two small children, a servant, two adults and perhaps the occasional visitor would certainly have restricted space in the little house. It has been assumed by past biographers that John Dickens had to leave Mile End Terrace because he could not afford the rent. Knowing of his difficulties with money later in life, they were no doubt eager to see the earliest possible signs of impending failure. However, the only fact used to support their hindsight was that John Dickens spent £35 a year on rent, yet had an income of only £110 per annum; this is totally inaccurate. His income between 1809 and 1812 increased each year, from £201 in 1809 to £226 in 1812. This was a substantial salary and one that quite justified a rent of £35.

Whatever the reason for a move from Mile End Terrace, the changeover seems to have been very smooth, with John Dickens' name being deemed a worthwhile selling point by his former landlord. The tenancy ended on 24 June 1812, and during my research I uncovered the following advertisement, which appeared in the *Hampshire Courier* on 22 and 29 June (see Plate 2):

MILE END TERRACE
FOR SALE, with immediate Possession, all that
modern well built DWELLING-HOUSE, situate as
above, late in the occupation of Mr. John Dickens. The
House comprises, in the basement, a good kitchen and cellar;
ground floor, two excellent parlours; first floor, two good
bed chambers, and two garrets in the attic. The whole replete with fixtures. The Premises are 18 feet in width, and
120 feet in depth.
    For further Particulars apply to Mr. WM. PEARCE,
Mile End.

The tenancy was taken up by a colleague of John Dickens at the Pay Office called Cobb, who later alluded to the many happy hours he had spent in the house while the Dickens family lived there.[25]

HAWKE STREET

There is no documentary evidence to indicate the whereabouts of the Dickens family's new home after moving from Mile End Terrace. John Dickens' name does not appear in the Portsmouth rate books for this period. The earliest reference to the next address appeared in 1891, in the second edition of Robert Langton's book *The Childhood and Youth of Charles Dickens*. He wrote:

'Of the infancy of Charles Dickens at Portsea little can now be known; it is, however, certain that in June quarter 1812 Mr. John Dickens left Mile-end Terrace and went to reside in Hawke Street, Portsea . . . Captain Henry James, R.N., writes me (June 1885): 'The chief recollection I have of the family of Mr. Dickens was in 1812. They had left the house in which the great man was born, and I once saw the babe in long petticoats in their lodging in Portsea'.[26]

Also published in 1891 was W. R. Hughes' book *A Week's Tramp in Dickens-land*, in which William Pearce the younger reported that on leaving his father's house the Dickens family moved into Hawke Street.[27]

Neither Langton nor Hughes indicated a house number, but fourteen years later Frederic G. Kitton followed up these clues with the following information:

A letter sent by me to the Portsmouth newspapers having reference to this subject brought me into communication with a Southsea lady, who informs me that an old gentleman of her acquaintance (an octogenarian) lived in his youth at No. 8, Hawke Street, and he clearly remembers that the Dickens family resided at No. 16. Hawke Street, in those days, he says, was a most respectable locality, the tenants being people of a good class, while there were superior lodging-houses for naval officers who desired to be within easy reach of their ships in the royal dockyard, distant about five minutes walk.[28]

The rate books for that period show that Hawke Street (at that time there was no 'e' on the end of Hawk) contained sixty houses, which ranged in rentable value from only £4 per annum up to

£15. Number 16 was rated at £10. These figures must be doubled to find a more true rent, if comparison is to be made with Mile End Terrace (where, as I have shown, the rentable value was listed in the rate books as £18 per annum, yet John Dickens paid £35). There was therefore little saving on rent, and it is possible that the move was made out of convenience, not necessity. It was certainly more convenient for access to John Dickens' work, the Navy Pay Office being just around the corner, two minutes away.

Number 16 was part of a terrace, having three floors and a basement and possibly giving more room to the growing family. However, John Dickens does not appear as a rate-payer (the rate-payer at number 16 was called Tyrer), confirming the report of Langton's correspondent that he held the status of lodger at Hawke Street, a status deemed much higher then than it is today and quite correct for people of good social standing.

References to this period, probably to the house in Hawke Street, were made by Dickens later in life. He confided to James T. Fields, as an example of his good memory, that when drawing the character of Mrs Pipchin in *Dombey and Son* he had in mind the lodging-house keeper in an English watering place where he was living with his father and mother when he was two years old. His sister Fanny commented on the description: 'Good Heavens! what does this mean? you have painted our lodging-house keeper, and you were but two years old at that time!'[29] These statements do present some conflict of opinion, since Dickens also wrote (in his fragment of autobiography) that Mrs Pipchin was drawn from Ellen Roylance, with whom he lodged in 1824. The two lodging-house keepers could not have been the same person, since the character sketch is remarked upon for being based on a memory from the age of two, not twelve, years of age. The logical conclusion is that Mrs Pipchin was created from two originals, not one.

The area of Hawke Street today contrasts sharply with its appearance in the nineteenth century. Built about 1780, the Dickens' home survived until the second world war, when it suffered damage from bombs and, like almost all the houses in the street, had to be demolished, later to be replaced by blocks of flats. The past atmosphere of the area must now be squeezed from the few photographs that exist. The deeds to the property are held by City of Portsmouth, and the period of Dickens' residence there is now recognised by a plaque on the wall of the

George Inn, placed there in 1986. The Dickens family probably stayed at their lodgings in Hawke Street for about eighteen months, until Christmas 1813, at which time they moved across Portsmouth to the developing area of Southsea.

39 WISH STREET

Southsea began its development at about the time of the battle of Trafalgar, as an extension of Portsmouth just outside the city ramparts. It comprised many substantial houses, particularly in the fashionable Terraces, and several streets of quite modest properties. Throughout its early development it maintained a rural character; and into this attractive, growing area moved the Dickens family.

Their residence in Wish Street can be substantiated with greater certainty than that at Hawke Street. Just as the birth of Charles was announced in the local newspapers, so too was the birth of their third child, Alfred Allen Dickens, born, they announced, at Southsea on 28 March 1814.[30] Church records indicate that he was baptised at St Mary's, Kingston, on 22 April, and that the address for the Dickens family was Wish Street. An entry in the rate book dated 3 September 1814 pinpoints the Dickens' home at number 39, a house with a rentable value of £20 per annum, double that of 16 Hawke Street and slightly higher than Mile End Terrace.

A search through the local newspapers around the calculated date of the Dickens' move uncovered the following advertisement, which is quite possibly the very same one that John Dickens saw:

ISLAND OF PORTSEA. To be LET or SOLD by PRIVATE CONTRACT, a very commodious and well-built FREEHOLD HOUSE and PREMISES, situated in Wish-street, leading to Southsea Common; comprising two good parlours, four bed rooms, with a good cellar, kitchen, yard, etc. and from its situation is remarkably well suited for the residence of a private family, with immediate possession. For further details apply to Mr Honeybourn, Builder, Portsea.[31]

The decision to move to what was clearly a better house, and to an attractive new location, may well have been influenced by the appearance of Elizabeth Dickens' sister Mary Allen. She had married in May 1812 but her husband, Thomas Allen, was killed at sea on 31 October 1813, and soon afterwards she went to live with the Dickens family, probably remaining a part of the family for the next eight years. The new baby, Alfred, was given his aunt's surname as a middle name.

Later that year, during the Michaelmas quarter of 1814, John Dickens was promoted again, this time to 11th Assistant Clerk, and things appeared to be going particularly well for the family: besides the promotion they were now living in a good house in an area altogether superior to that of Hawke Street, Mary Allen had joined them, bringing with her a pension of £50 a year, and they had a new baby in the family.

The address at Wish Street has received very little attention from biographers, yet the Dickens family lived there for about a year. At this time Charles was between two and three years old, and likely to have remembered later events relating to this period. It seems most likely that he referred to this time when he spoke to John Forster:

> He has often told me that he remembered the small front garden to the house at Portsea, from which he was taken away when he was two years old, and where, watched by a nurse through a low kitchen-window almost level with the gravel walk, he trotted about with something to eat, and his little elder sister with him.[32]

Another incident remembered by the adult Dickens also refers, it seems likely, to this period, probably to the new year of 1814:

> New Year's Day. What Party can that have been, and what New Year's Day can that have been, which first rooted the phrase, 'A New Year's Day Party,' in my mind? So far back do my recollections of childhood extend, that I have a vivid remembrance of the sensation of being carried down-stairs in a woman's arms, and holding tight to her, in the terror of seeing the steep perspective below. Hence, I may have been carried into this Party, for anything I know; but, somehow or other, I most certainly got there, and was in a doorway looking on; and in that look a New Year's Party revealed itself to me, as a very long row of ladies and gentlemen sitting against a wall, all

drinking at once out of little glass cups with handles, like custard-cups. What can this Party have been! I am afraid it must have been a dull one, but I *know* it came off. Where can this Party have been! I have not the faintest notion where, but I am absolutely certain it was somewhere. Why the company should all have been drinking at once, and especially why they should all have been drinking out of custard-cups, are points of fact over which the Waters of Oblivion have long rolled. I doubt if they can have been drinking the Old Year out and the New One in, because they were not at supper and had no table before them. There was no speech-making, no quick movement and change of action, no demonstration of any kind. They were all sitting in a long row against the wall – very like my first idea of the good people in Heaven, as I derived it from a wretched picture in a Prayer-book – and they had all got their heads a little thrown back, and were all drinking at once. It is possible enough that I, the baby, may have been caught up out of bed to have a peep at the company, and that the company may happen to have been thus occupied for the flash and space of a moment only. But, it has always seemed to me as if I looked at them for a long time – hours – during which they did nothing else; and to this present time, a casual mention in my hearing, of a Party on a New Year's Day, always revives that picture.[33]

A further probable reference to this period is recorded in another article, in which Dickens dreams of a figure from the past:

It is a figure that I once saw, just after dark, chalked upon a door in a little back lane near a country church – my first church. How young a child I may have been at the time I don't know, but it horrified me so intensely – in connection with the churchyard, I suppose, for it smokes a pipe, and has a big hat with each of its ears sticking out in a horizontal line under the brim, and is not in itself more oppressive than a mouth from ear to ear, a pair of goggle eyes, and hands like two bunches of carrots, five in each, can make it – that it is still vaguely alarming to me to recall (as I have often done before, lying awake) the running home, the looking behind, the horror of its following me; though whether disconnected from the door, or door and all, I can't say, and perhaps never could. It lays a disagreeable train.[34]

Another 'looking back' incident occurred in 1866, when Dickens visited Portsmouth on a reading tour. The manager of his tours at that time, George Dolby, later recalled the occasion in a book he wrote about Dickens:

> In the hope that the sea breezes might have the effect of relieving Mr. Dickens of the cold from which he was still suffering, we decided to visit Southsea before the Portsmouth reading. And here two amusing incidents occurred.
>
> On the morning after our arrival we set out for a walk, and turning the corner of a street suddenly, found ourselves in Landport Terrace. The name of the street catching Mr. Dickens's eye, he suddenly exclaimed, 'By Jove! here is the place where I was born'; and, acting on his suggestion, we walked up and down the terrace for some time, speculating as to which of the houses had the right to call itself his cradle. Beyond a recollection that there was a small front garden to the house he had no idea of the place for he was only two years old when his father was removed to London from Portsmouth. As the houses were nearly all alike, and each had a small front garden, we were not much helped in our quest by Mr. Dickens's recollections, and great was the laughter at his humorous conjectures. He must have lived in one house because 'it looked so like his father'; another one must have been his home because it looked like the birthplace of a man who had deserted it; a third was very like the cradle of a puny, weak youngster such as he had been; and so on, through the row. According to his own account, Southsea had not contributed much to his physical strength, neither indeed had Chatham . . . But as none of the houses in Landport Terrace could cry out and say, as he recounted these facts, 'That boy was born here!' the mystery remained unsolved, and we passed on.[35]

Biographers have assumed that Dickens knew the street in which he was born, even if he did not know the house, and that Dolby got the name of the street wrong – that is, he meant Mile End Terrace, Landport, not Landport Terrace. However, it would not be surprising if Dickens did not know where he was born, since he was only five months old when taken from there. But Wish Street he would have remembered more easily. This is supported by Dolby's report that they were walking in Southsea (Mile End Terrace is about a mile and a quarter distant from Southsea) and the fact that Landport Terrace runs into Wish Street. The Dickens home was just a few steps from Landport Terrace. The small front garden mentioned by Dolby echoes Forster, as mentioned earlier.

Sometime during 1814 the family received bad news from London, where John Dickens' colleague in the Pay Office, his wife's brother Thomas Barrow, had fallen from a Hackney coach while alighting in the courtyard of Somerset House and had broken his leg; it was an accident that was to dog him for the rest of his life. But worse followed: the happiness of the Dickens family at their new home was severely jolted in September 1814, when tragedy struck with the death of the new baby. The newspapers once again carried their two-line report:

Died, on Tuesday last, at Southsea, of water on the brain, the infant son of Mr. Dickens.[36]

For some as yet undiscovered reason the child was buried in the parish of Widley, about five miles to the north of Southsea.[37]

John Dickens was recalled to work at Somerset House soon after, on 1 January 1815.[38] The previous year had seen the defeat of Napoleon and the end of the war with America, so work in the Portsmouth dockyards was being reduced. John Dickens may have been somewhat disappointed by the move: he had recently received promotion, was enjoying his highest ever income at £231 a year – which would reduce to £200 in London[39] – and had only that year settled into a comfortable house in Southsea. This was a lot to lose; and yet he may also have been thankful to leave behind the sad memory of a dead child.

Wish Street, which had its name changed in the nineteenth century to Kings Road, has undergone two major changes of character since the Dickens family lived there in 1814. By the end of the nineteenth century it had changed from the quiet residential, semi-rural setting of John Dickens' day to an extremely busy and flourishing commercial thoroughfare. Then, like Hawke Street, it too suffered damage in the second world war and became primarily the setting for blocks of flats, one of which now covers the site of Dickens' home. The period of Dickens' residence is not recognised.

It is interesting to note that two other giants of English literature had connections with this small Southsea street. In 1882 H. G. Wells served an apprenticeship in Hide's drapery shop in Kings Road; and from 1882 to 1890 Conan Doyle had a doctor's practice at number 1 Bush Villas, just at the end of Kings Road: it was here that he first started writing his Sherlock Holmes stories.

John Dickens may well have reflected, on the coach journey from Portsmouth to London, on the eventful seven and a half years he had spent in one of the country's most important dockyard towns – eventful both for him and for the country, and, little though he would have thought it, for the future of English literature. His little boy though, sitting beside him in the coach, carried few memories: his small front garden, soldiers exercising, his lodging-house keeper, a chalk figure in a country lane, a new year's party and the fact that they came away in the snow.

2
London 1815–16

The two years spent in London by the Dickens family at this time is the most difficult of all periods to document. Past biographers have dismissed it lightly: Forster gives just one sentence, Johnson one paragraph, and Langton mentions it not at all. On the evidence presented in the past it might be questioned if the Dickens family lived in London at all during this period. Yet some documentary material does exist.

The period spent in the capital was exactly two years, and this can be confirmed by reference to Admiralty records, which show that John Dickens was paid no 'Outport Allowance' between 1 January 1815 and 31 December 1816.[1] He was at this time earning about £200 a year – a good salary, but less than the £231 he had been receiving while at Portsmouth. John Dickens' workplace in London, and the headquarters of the Navy Pay Office, was at Somerset House in the Strand, a large and impressive building erected only 40 years before in 1775, but built upon the site of an old royal palace.

The family group probably still included Elizabeth's sister Mary Allen, who had joined them at Portsmouth and was still with them two years later in Chatham. Also a servant may well have been employed, as one was at Portsmouth, to help around the house and with the two children, but there is no record to say that this was so. During the Dickens family's two years in London the size of the family was increased with the birth of Letitia Mary Dickens, born on 23 April 1816. Her baptism is listed in the Register of Baptisms in the Parish of St Mary-le-bone[2] and indicates John Dickens' position in life as 'gentleman', with his address simply stated as St Marylebone.

NORFOLK STREET

An extensive search through the rate books of St Marylebone for the years 1815 and 1816 has failed to discover the name of John

Dickens (though there is listed his brother, William, whose wedding
to Miss Sarah Latham the Dickenses probably attended at St
George's, Hanover Square, on 28 December 1815).[3] It must be
assumed, then, that the family stayed in lodgings. The only
evidence for a more precise address than that given in the Register
of Baptisms comes from John Forster, who wrote: 'When his
father was again brought up by his duties to London from
Portsmouth, they went into lodgings in Norfolk-street, Middlesex
Hospital'.[4] Forster is often notoriously weak with details of
Dickens' early life, yet in the absence of other evidence his
information must at present be accepted. The rate books for 1815
and 1816 indicate that only one house in Norfolk Street was let to
tenants: that was number 19. It was owned by Richard Biddle and
rated at £45 per annum.

However, there is evidence to locate another address, since
many years later, in 1830, Charles Dickens was again in lodgings
in Norfolk Street and this time can be firmly located at number 10.
The owner or resident at number 10, running a grocer's shop
from the premises both in 1815–16 and 1830, was a gentleman by
the name of John Dodd. This man is a good strong link between
the Dickens family and the same address for the two different
periods; yet there is an even stronger tie drawing together John
Dodd and John Dickens over that span of fifteen years, for
Dodd it was who appeared in the list of creditors when John
Dickens was arrested for debt in 1824.[5] They must therefore have
been known to each other prior to 1830. This debt between John
Dickens and John Dodd would perhaps be a good reason for
Dodd *not* to accept the Dickens family as lodgers some years later;
and yet the two men may well have had much in common, since
Dodd was himself arrested for debt in November 1823, being
released three months later; and in December 1826 he was
declared a bankrupt, obtaining a discharge two months after that.
It is not difficult to imagine John Dodd and John Dickens sharing
anecdotes of their unfortunate predicaments. Indeed, is it possible
that the attitude towards money of one of this pair led the other
astray?

This must be considered, since it may well be that John Dickens
first experienced difficulty with money soon after moving to
London. Throughout his career with the Navy Pay Office he had
earned a gradual rise in salary from about £78 a year to about
£231. In April 1815, having completed ten years of service, he

received a rise in basic salary from £140 to £200; however, this was more than offset by his loss of 'Outport Allowances', leaving him with a net loss of £47 that year and £31 in 1816. Under these circumstances the situation might well have developed where he needed to beg or borrow money. In her will the mother of John Dickens, who also conveniently lived in St Marylebone, left less money to him than to his brother William, the reason being, she noted, that John had received sums of money from her 'some years ago'.[6] Since the will was written in 1824 and the Dickenses had been living in Chatham between 1817 and 1822, the best opportunities to beg such sums would have fallen during 1815–16.

This is the best time, too, from which Charles could have had his first recollections of this grandmother. As housekeeper to the Crewe family Elizabeth Dickens was remembered by the children of that house as an excellent storyteller. It would seem that Charles remembered her too, as he wrote in *The Holly Tree Inn*.

My first impressions of an Inn, dated from the Nursery; consequently, I went back to the Nursery for a starting-point, and found myself at the knee of a sallow woman with a fishy eye, an aquiline nose, and a green gown, whose speciality was a dismal narrative of a landlord by the roadside, whose visitors unaccountably disappeared, for many years, until it was discovered that the pursuit of his life had been to convert them into pies . . . I had no sooner disposed of this criminal than there started up another of the same period, whose profession was, originally, housebreaking; in the pursuit of which art he had his right ear chopped off one night as he was burglariously getting in at a window, by a brave and lovely servant-maid (whom the aquiline-nosed woman, though not at all answering the description, always mysteriously implied to be herself). After several years, this brave and lovely servant-maid was married to the landlord of a country Inn: which landlord had this remarkable characteristic, that he always wore a silk nightcap, and never would, on any consideration, take it off. At last, one night, when he was fast asleep, the brave and lovely woman lifted up his silk nightcap on the right side, and found that he had no ear there; upon which, she sagaciously perceived that he was the clipped housebreaker, who had married her with the intention of putting her to death. She immediately heated the poker and terminated his career, for which she was taken to King George upon his throne, and received the compliments of royalty on her great discretion and valour. This same narrator, who had a Ghoulish pleasure, I have long been persuaded, in terrifying me to the utmost confines of my reason, had another authentic anecdote within her own experience, founded, I now believe, upon Raymond and Agnes or the Bleeding Nun. She said it happened to her brother-in-law, who was immensely rich – which my father was not; and immensely tall – which my father was not. It was always a point with this Ghoule to present my dearest relations and friends to my youthful mind, under circumstances of disparaging contrast.[7]

The probability that the narrator of these stories was Elizabeth Dickens is supported in a number of ways: (1) the chronology of the article places this anecdote before the Chatham days and when the child was of nursery age, which Dickens was in 1815/16; (2) Charles then lived very close to his grandmother; (3) his grandmother was well remembered as a storyteller; (4) the woman in the story describes herself as having been a servant-maid, as had Elizabeth Dickens been; and (5) the woman particularly ran down the child's father and close friends and relatives, which Elizabeth Dickens is known to have done to John Dickens.

A second article by the adult Dickens would also seem to refer to his grandmother at this time.

I remember to have been taken, upon a New Year's Day, to the Bazaar in Soho Square, London, to have a present bought for me. A distinct impression yet lingers in my soul that a grim and unsympathetic old personage of the female gender, flavoured with musty dry lavender, dressed in black crape, and wearing a pocket in which something clinked at my ear as we went along, conducted me on this occasion to the World of Toys. I remember to have been incidentally escorted a little way down some conveniently retired street diverging from Oxford Street, for the purpose of being shaken; and nothing has ever slaked the burning thirst for vengeance awakened in me by this female's manner of insisting upon wiping my nose herself (I had a cold and a pocket-handkerchief), on the screw principle. For many years I was unable to excogitate the reason why she should have undertaken to make me a present. In the exercise of a matured judgment, I have now no doubt that she had done something bad in her youth, and that she took me out as an act of expiation.

Nearly lifted off my legs by this adamantine woman's grasp of my glove (another fearful invention of those dark ages – a muffler, and fastened at the wrist like a handcuff), I was haled through the Bazaar. My tender imagination (or conscience) represented certain small apartments in corners, resembling wooden cages, wherein I have since seen reason to suppose that ladies' collars and the like are tried on, as being, either dark places of confinement for refractory youth, or dens in which the lions were kept who fattened on boys who said they didn't care. Suffering tremendous terrors from the vicinity of these avenging mysteries, I was put before the expanse of toys, apparently about a hundred and twenty acres in extent, and was asked what I would have to the value of half-a-crown? Having first selected every object at half-a-guinea, and then staked all the aspirations of my nature on every object at five shillings, I hit, as a last resource, upon a Harlequin's Wand – painted particoloured, like the Harlequin himself.

Although of a highly hopeful and imaginative temperament, I had no fond belief that the possession of this talisman would enable me to change Mrs. Pipchin at my side into anything agreeable. When I tried the effect of the wand upon her, behind her bonnet, it was rather as a desperate experiment founded on the conviction that she could change into nothing worse, than with any latent hope that she would change into something better. Howbeit, I clung to the delusion that when I got home I should do something magical with this wand; and I did not resign all hope of it until I had, by many trials, proved the wand's total incapacity. It had no effect on the staring obstinacy of a rocking-horse; it produced no live Clown out of the hot beefsteak-pie at dinner; it could not even influence the minds of my honoured parents to the extent of suggesting the decency and propriety of their giving me an invitation to sit up at supper.[8]

The adult Dickens has provided us with very little information on his paternal grandmother, yet if these two articles are relevant they give a sharp, if limited, description. She was grim and unsympathetic; a sallow woman with a fishy eye and aquiline nose, sometimes dressed in black crape, with a flavour of musty dry lavender about her. At this time she would have been aged about seventy. She was a good storyteller and always made a point of making disparaging remarks about Charles' friends and relatives, particularly his father. If these were the impressions left upon the small child, then it must be conceded that visits to Grandma were not an altogether happy experience. Of course if his father were continuously begging loans and his grandmother resented this, then the general atmosphere in the family would not have been conducive to friendly relationships.

Whatever the financial situation, little Charles remembered little or nothing of it. Nor did he remember the area in which they lived. It was a growing part of London; the Middlesex Hospital itself had expanded from quite humble beginnings, though it had not yet reached the proportions it was to achieve in the 1830s. Norfolk Street was newly named, having been previously known as Green Lane, when it led out from London towards the countryside of Camden Town and Somers Town. In 1814 the elegant Fitzroy Square, further up Norfolk Street from number 10, was built but still open on one side; and Tottenham Court Road was an attractive busy thoroughfare, though it still had its turnpike and its farms behind the houses.

Close examination of the area close to Norfolk Street at that time makes it possible to plot the second point in the pattern of John Dickens' theatrical connections. In Tottenham Street, at the corner of which stood 10 Norfolk Street, was situated the Theatre of Variety. This was run from 1814 by a man called Brierley, who, even with Covent Garden experience behind him and £6000 to spend on the building, was unable to make a financial success of it and moved on in 1821. The choice of new year's day gift from his grandmother shows that the very young Charles was already well acquainted with harlequins, and such an attraction as the Theatre of Variety just around the corner must surely have drawn Mr and Mrs Dickens.

Norfolk Street itself comprised 34 dwellings, attracting respectable ratable values between £30 and £50. Number 10, a large building on four floors, shared the distinction with three others of being rated at the highest value. The building had its address changed in 1867 to 22 Cleveland Street, and has survived with that address to the present day. John Dodd's grocery shop has been changed into a café, and the rooms above, where the

Dickens family lived, are still let out to tenants. It is one of the few buildings left in London that was lived in by Charles Dickens, yet no plaque indicates its distinction.

Admiralty records indicate that John Dickens was moved from London on 1 January 1817. He was no doubt relieved at the prospect of an increased salary in a less expensive part of the country.

3

Sheerness and Chatham

SHEERNESS

When John Dickens was moved from his post at Somerset House it seems likely that his initial destination was Sheerness in Kent: several early writers on Dickens report a short period there, but later biographers let the matter drop. The earliest reference came in 1852, when a book called *The Men of the Time in 1852, or, Sketches of Living Notables*[1] reported the following anecdote:

> the father of 'Boz' was at times fond of dilating upon the strange scenes he had witnessed. One of his stories described a sitting-room he once enjoyed at Blue-town, Sheerness, abutting on the theatre. Of an evening he used to sit in this room, and could hear what was passing on the stage, and join in the chorus of 'God Save the King', and 'Britannia rules the Waves,' – then the favourite songs of Englishmen.

John Dickens' next door neighbour was almost certainly the Sheerness Theatre, situated at the corner of Victory Street and the High Street. It was leased from 1807 to December 1816 to Samuel Jerrold, father of Douglas Jerrold and grandfather of Blanchard Jerrold, both of whom Charles Dickens was to know later in life. In 1816 the land on which the theatre stood (indeed, the complete length of one side of the High Street) was needed for expansion of the dockyard, but since the enclosing walls were not completed until 1821 it seems likely that the theatre survived a few months more, long enough at least for the Dickens family to be exhilarated by their neighbour. A biography of his father by Blanchard Jerrold gives a valuable insight into life at the Sheerness Theatre:

> The Blue Town, Sheerness, was crammed with sailors and their officers. The spirit of recent great achievements animated them; and to Mr. Jerrold's little wooden theatre in High Street flocked officers and men, in sufficient crowds to make the manager's

speculation for many years highly lucrative. The audience was not, as may be readily imagined, a very quiet one. Still, *Hamlet*, and *Richard the Third*, and *Macbeth* drew houses; but pieces having some reference to nautical life, and farces, broad rather than elegant, interspersed with old comic songs, were the chief elements of the usual entertainment.[2]

Following the end of the war Sheerness would have quietened down by the time John Dickens arrived, even though an enormous rebuilding programme in the dockyard had been put into operation. Nevertheless it must have been exciting for the Dickens family to live next door to a theatre, even though Sheerness was not as a whole very attractive.

The town stood in a very flat locality, below the level of the sea at high-water mark, and was only prevented from being flooded and uninhabitable by a strongly-built sea wall which defended it to the east, north and south. The flat land behind Mile Town and Blue Town formed an area of about 1700 acres and was then the receptacle of the town sullage. It was intersected by watercourses which carried with them a great proportion of the town sewage, emitting health-destroying malaria, saturating the earth and polluting the air. In fact Sheerness was nearly surrounded, except seaward, by stagnant and stinking ditches, the principal of which were primarily formed for the purpose of draining the town and the marshes themselves but, for want of a proper and efficient outlet, had become reservoirs and hotbeds for the generation of poisonous matter, producing disease and death. The town itself was uninteresting: the somewhat irregularly-built main street – which had a number of side streets, with narrow cross-streets behind them – comprised wooden houses, small shops and numerous taverns, and made a dull and dismal high street.[3]

Later biographers may well have considered John Dickens' association with Sheerness as that only of a visitor, knowing that visits were made there from Chatham shortly afterwards. However, it seems unlikely that such visits would have necessitated the taking of lodgings; and the Sheerness Theatre could not have survived much beyond the early part of 1817. The Dickens family's stay in Sheerness was very short. A local newspaper, the *Kentish Chronicle*, reported that on 25 March 1817 reductions were made in the number of clerks employed in the dockyard offices at Sheerness and Chatham, with seven clerks at Sheerness being

discharged. It seems likely that, at this time of major adjustment
of staff, John Dickens was moved along the coast to the dockyard
at Chatham.

CHATHAM

The Dickens family arrived in Chatham in the first week of April
1817, and their reaction to the move from Sheerness – a move
from a town of only 800 people to one of 24 000 – may well have
been similar to that of R. G. Hobbes, a navy clerk who was also
appointed to both towns; he wrote that Chatham 'indicated a new
life to me, a life of complete change from that at Sheerness – then
isolated almost beyond the endurance of many – to a bustling
town, or rather, group of towns, and a cathedral city, together
with a comparative nearness to London'.[4]

Perhaps, on removal to Chatham, the family were presented
with the same prospect of the town as Dickens later created for
his *alter ego* David Copperfield: 'Chatham – which, in that night's
aspect, is a mere dream of chalk, and drawbridges, and mastless
ships, in a muddy river, roofed like Noah's arks'.[5] A closer look
was given by Dickens through the words of Mr Pickwick:

'The principal productions of these towns,' says Mr. Pickwick,
'appear to be soldiers, sailors, Jews, chalk, shrimps, officers, and
dockyard men. The commodities chiefly exposed for sale in the
public streets are marine stores, hard-bake, apples, flat-fish,
and oysters. The streets present a lively and animated
appearance, occasioned chiefly by the conviviality of the
military. It is truly delightful to a philanthropic mind, to see
these gallant men staggering along under the influence of an
overflow, both of animal and ardent spirits; more especially
when we remember that the following them about, and jesting
with them, affords a cheap and innocent amusement for the
boy population . . .

'The consumption of tobacco in these towns (continues Mr.
Pickwick) must be very great; and the smell which pervades the
streets must be exceedingly delicious to those who are extremely
fond of smoking.'[6]

Dickens' tongue-in-cheek view of Chatham – and in particular
of its military population, which in 1820 comprised five regiments

of soldiers and a battery of artillery, besides its naval personnel –
glosses over a reckless and hazardous aspect of the town, as
indicated in this extract from R. G. Hobbes:

> The want of healthful recreation for soldiers and sailors which
> we noticed at Sheerness was much more evident here, and the
> very name of a soldier or sailor seemed identified with
> drunkenness and debauchery. The men seemed to have
> nowhere to go but to the canteen or public-house; and street
> rows and midnight brawls appeared to be far more frequent, as
> might be expected from the strength of the garrison, than at
> Sheerness. Chatham has been called 'the wickedest place in the
> world'.[7]

At this period, it is worth noting, there was a daily rum allowance
in the navy of a half pint per person.[8] But the very danger on the
street was just one ingredient of Chatham's general excitement;
there was a constant bustle in the town, with soldiers and brass
bands marching off to Gravesend and detachments returning
from abroad, marching through to bands and cheering people.
The recruiting sergeant, bringing in a long retinue of recruits from
all parts of the country, was one of Chatham's most frequent
sights. The recruits were generally a somewhat shabby lot:
agricultural labourers, seedy clerks, broken-down tradesmen and
sometimes a gentleman's runaway son or two, or an abandoned
roué.[9]

A market was held every Saturday and two annual fairs each
ran for three days, one in May and the other in September.
During August people of every rank and station flocked in from
the surrounding countryside and business was almost totally
suspended when, for two days, horse races were held on the
Lines. In November two Saints' Days were celebrated: on St
Catherine's Eve, 24 November, a boy was dressed up to represent
the saint and was carried around the streets, with pipe and drum
going before, by ropemakers' apprentices, who collected largesse
for a supper; and similar entertainment was provided by the
blacksmiths' apprentices two days before, on St Clement's Eve,
with a youth disguised in a mask and wig as an old man and
carried in a chair of state: speeches were made, rhymes read and
money collected. Dickens later referred to the blacksmiths' saint
in a work song that he had Joe Gargery, Old Orlick and Pip

singing in *Great Expectations*, a song he picked up, probably, from an occasion such as this. Other celebrations round the town were made on 1 May by chimneysweeps, on 2 May by milkmaids and on Christmas Eve by mummers, progressing from house to house singing and collecting money.

The town contained a number of schools and churches – but even more public-houses; there was a post office in the High Street and one delivery a day was made by the sole postman; coaches ran from Chatham each way along the London to Dover road – still at that time a favourite haunt of highwaymen – and boats carried traffic to London as well as to Sheerness on each tide. Shopkeepers used paper sparingly: buyers of flour took a wooden box and pieces of meat were carried home on a wooden skewer. Bakers sent out bread in covered trucks drawn by dogs, which practice caused many accidents through horses taking fright, and the custom was later stopped by an Act of Parliament.[10] Into this rough and busy town moved the genteel Dickens family, looking for accommodation that would suit their position in life.

ORDNANCE TERRACE

Scanning the newspapers for a likely new residence, John Dickens probably saw the following advertisement (see Plate 6):

VALUABLE FREEHOLD ESTATES.
LAND TAX REDEEMED.
TO BE SOLD BY AUCTION,
By Mr. T. WILKINSON.
ON THURSDAY, April 10, 1817, at the MITRE
TAVERN, Chatham, between the hours of six and
eight o'clock in the evening, (subject to such conditions as
will be then and there produced.)
  All that valuable brick built DWELLING HOUSE, with
yard and garden, beautifully situated at Ordnance Place,
fronting the road to Fort Pitt, commanding beautiful views
of the surrounding country, and fit for the residence of a gen-
teel family.
  Together with all those four brick built DWELLING
HOUSES, near the same, called Union Place, with five
other Dwelling Houses, part fronting Fort Pitt-street, the

whole of which are let to respectable tenants at will, and may be viewed any time previous to the Sale by leave of the Tenants, and Particulars known by application to the AUCTIONEER, St. Margaret's Bank, Rochester.[11]

Rate books show that the Dickens family lived at the second house in the row (later to become 2 Ordnance Terrace) at least from the end of December 1817 (but probably from April 1817) until the beginning of April 1821, and that the ratable value was £16 per annum, later reduced to £15 10s.[12] It was at this time one of only four houses in the terrace, a fifth being added some time between 1818 and 1820, and the others coming along even later. For verification of the address Langton says that in 1883 there were probably ten or twelve persons living who could remember the family occupying this house.[13]

Like the birthplace of Dickens at Portsmouth, this first home in Chatham was a new, pleasant, typically Georgian-style building. The narrow hall was lit by a fanlight over the front door and had leading from it a small living and dining room, which looked out over the roadway. The best-parlour room was on the first floor, together with the main bedroom. Two smaller attic bedrooms were situated at the top of the house, the front one having a splendid view over the lower town and the river. There was a kitchen, cellar and small living room in the basement.

Pleasant though the house was, it must have been rather cramped for the Dickens family: besides John and Elizabeth Dickens the family comprised Mary Allen, Fanny, Charles, Letitia and two servants, Mary Weller and Jane Bonny. Over the next three years two more children were born into the Dickens family, Harriet (baptised 3 September 1819) and Frederick (baptised 4 August 1820).[14] It seems likely that one of the attic rooms would have been used as a nursery bedroom for all the children, as was usual in the nineteenth century, while Aunt Mary (called Fanny by the children) would have slept in the other attic bedroom. The two servants would have occupied the living room in the basement and must have made an odd couple, Jane Bonny being described by Langton as an old lady[15] and Mary Weller being just thirteen years old.

CHARLES DICKENS' CHILDHOOD AT CHATHAM

However this crowded family organised itself, it seems to have been well-ordered and happy. Charles remembered that his mother taught him regularly every day for a long time, including the rudiments of English and Latin. Forster relates that, five years before the words were written in *David Copperfield*, Dickens had told him: 'I faintly remember her teaching me the alphabet; and when I look upon the fat black letters in the primer, the puzzling novelty of their shapes, and the easy good nature of O and S, always seem to present themselves before me as they used to do'.[16] According to Mary Weller, Aunt Mary also used to help with Charles' education,[17] and he was convinced that he was taught thoroughly well.[18]

Daily exercise with Mary Weller was part of the routine too. Mrs E. Davey, with whom John and Elizabeth Dickens lived just prior to his death, recalled an anecdote told her by Charles' mother:

> Once when Charles was a tiny boy, and the family were down at Chatham, the nurse had a great deal of trouble in inducing him to follow her when out for his daily walk. When they returned home, Mrs. Dickens said to her, 'Well, how have the children behaved?' 'Very nicely indeed, ma'am – all but Master Charley.' 'What has he done?' 'Why ma'am he will insist in always going the same road every day.' 'Charley, Charley, how is this?' 'Why, mamma,' answered the urchin, 'does not the Bible say we must walk in the same path all the days of our life?'[19]

Precocious as this may seem, Charles was generally remembered as 'a lively boy of a good, genial, open disposition, and not quarrelsome, as most children are at times'.[20] He described his own appearance thus: 'I date from the period when small boys had a dreadful high-shouldered sleeved strait-waistcoat put upon them by their keepers, over which their dreadful little trousers were buttoned tight, so that they roamed about disconsolate, with their hands in their pockets'.[21]

Despite such confined, disconsolate moments there was much fun in the young boy's life, the general tenor of the household being set, no doubt, by his father, who was described in Chatham as 'a fellow of infinite humour, chatty, lively, and agreeable'.[22] There was much singing in the household, so much so that Fanny and Charles became proficient enough to be a prize attraction for John Dickens to show off. They would sing songs – many of which Charles later recalled in his writings – at birthday parties, twelfth-night parties and ordinary evening parties, whether they were held at the Mitre Tavern in Chatham High Street, where John Dickens had become friendly with the landlord of the famous inn, at their own home, at other people's homes or in the hayfield in front of the Terrace, at picnics.[23] The Mitre was indeed a particular focal point in the social life of the Dickens family. John Tribe, the son of the landlord at this time, later recalled that Charles and Fanny were good entertainers, always being well applauded, and he recollected one particular duet performed at a party, Charles singing in a clear treble voice.[24] Charles himself later wrote:

> There was an Inn in the cathedral town where I went to school . . . It was the Inn where friends used to put up, and where we used to go to see parents, and to have salmon and fowls, and be tipped. It had an ecclesiastical sign – the Mitre – and a bar that seemed to be the next best thing to a bishopric, it was so snug. I loved the landlord's youngest daughter to distraction – but let that pass. It was in this Inn that I was cried over by my rosy little sister, because I had acquired a black eye in a fight.[25]

Besides their own singing, there was also the singing of Mary Weller, who sent the children off to sleep with the evening hymn.[26]

But not everything was quite so gay, nor all of Mary Weller's influence quite so soothing.[27] She was responsible for telling Charles a number of ghastly stories that set his imagination racing, including one about a Captain Murderer, who took lovely young brides in order to cut them up and cook them in a pie; this story he heard, he believed, hundreds of times, the nurse preceding each recital with a long low hollow groan and a clawing at the air with both hands.[28] Another story concerned a black cat: 'a weird and glaring-eyed supernatural Tom, who was reputed to prowl about the world by night, sucking the breath of infancy, and who was endowed with a special thirst (as I was given to understand) for mine'. Yet another concerned a plague of rats that pursued a dockyard shipwright, eventually eating him; and another featured an unearthly animal that appeared in the streets. All attempts by the young boy to dismiss the improbable stories with reason were firmly discredited by the nurse, and he suffered fear while awake and nightmares while asleep. His experiences with his nurse during the day were not always pleasant ones, either: in a description of a return to Chatham – described as Dullborough Town – he later wrote:

> in my very young days I was taken to so many layings-in that I wonder I escaped becoming a professional martyr to them in after-life. I suppose I had a very sympathetic nurse with a large circle of married acquaintance. However that was, as I continued my walk through Dullborough I found many houses to be solely associated in my mind with this particular interest. At one little greengrocer's shop, down certain steps from the street, I remembered to have waited on a lady who had four children (I am afraid to write five, though I fully believe it was five) at a birth. This meritorious woman held quite a reception in her room on the morning when I was introduced there, and the sight of the house brought vividly to mind how the four (five) deceased young people lay, side by side, on a clean cloth on a chest of drawers: reminding me by a homely association, which I suspect their complexion to have assisted, of pigs' feet as they are usually displayed at a neat tripe-shop.[29]

As an adult he wrote, 'If we all knew our own minds . . . I suspect we should find our nurses responsible for most of the dark corners we are forced to go back to, against our wills.'[30]

But ever-present though these horrors were, they did not overburden Charles, and he later remembered just as well the mischief that Mary Weller led him into:

> On what other early New Year's Day can I possibly have been an innocent accomplice in the secreting – in a coal cellar too – of a man with a wooden leg! There was no man with a wooden leg, in the circle of my acknowledged and lawful relations and friends. Yet, I clearly remember that we stealthily conducted the man with the wooden leg – whom we knew intimately – into the coal cellar, and that, in getting him over the coals to hide him behind some partition there was beyond, his wooden leg bored itself in among the small coals, and his hat flew off,

and he fell backward and lay prone: a spectacle of helplessness.
I clearly remember that his struggles to get up among the small
coals, and to obtain any purchase on himself in those slippery
and shifting circumstances, were a work of exceeding difficulty,
involving delay and noise that occasioned us excessive terror. I
have not the least idea who 'we' were, except that I had a little
sister for another innocent accomplice, and that there must
have been a servant girl for principal: neither do I know
whether the man with the wooden leg robbed the house, before
or afterwards, or otherwise nefariously distinguished himself.
Nor, how a cat came to be connected with the occasion, and
had a fit, and ran over the top of a door. But, I know that some
awful reason compelled us to hush it all up, and that we 'never
told'. For many years, I had this association with a New Year's
Day entirely to myself, until at last, the anniversary being come
round again, I said to the little sister, as she and I sat by chance
among our children, 'Do you remember the New Year's Day of
the man with the wooden leg?' Whereupon, a thick black
curtain which had overhung him from her infancy, went up,
and she saw just this much of the man, and not a jot more.[31]

Outside the house his hours of play were remembered as
carefree and imaginative. Opposite Ordnance Terrace there was a
playing field; it had, he later remembered, two beautiful hawthorn
trees, a hedge, turf and buttercups and daisies:

Here in the haymaking time, had I been delivered from the
dungeons of Seringapatan, an immense pile (of haycock), by
my countrymen, the victorious British (boy next door and his
two cousins), and had been recognized with ecstasy by my
affianced one (Miss Green), who had come all the way from
England (second house in the terrace) to ransom me, and marry
me. Here had I first heard in confidence, from one whose father
was greatly connected, being under Government, of the
existence of a terrible banditti called 'The Radicals', whose
principles were that the Prince Regent wore stays and that
nobody had a right to any salary, and that the army and navy
ought to be put down – horrors at which I trembled in my bed,
after supplicating that the Radicals might be speedily taken and
hanged.[32]

Perhaps his awe of the Prince Regent was nourished by his mother, who took him to see the prince as he passed through Rochester, standing him on a wall outside the theatre and making him cheer.[33] The Prince Regent and his stays seemed to have left a deep impression on the little boy, possibly because Charles connected him with the very first picture book that he owned:

The first picture-book! We date from the time of the Prince Regent, and remember picture-books about dandies – satires upon that eminent personage himself, possibly – but *we* never knew it. In those days there was a certain bright, smooth cover for picture-books, like a glorified surgical plaster. It has gone out this long, long time. The picture book that seems to have been our first, was about one Mr. Pillblister (in the medical professions, we presume, from the name), who gave a party. As the legend is impressed on our remembrance, it opened thus:

> Mr. Pillblister and Betsy his sister,
> Determined on giving a treat;
> Gay dandies they call
> To a supper and ball
> At their house in Great Camomile Street.

The pictures represented male dandies in every stage of preparation for this festival; holding on to bed-posts to have their stays laced; embellishing themselves with artificial graces of many kinds; and enduring various humiliations in remote garrets. One gentleman found a hole in his stocking at the last moment.

> A hole in my stocking,
> O how very shocking!
> Says poor Mr. (Some one) enraged.
> It's always my fate
> To be so very late,
> When at Mr. Pillblister's engaged![34]

The book was called *The Dandies Ball*, published in 1819 by John Marshall, and was sold for one shilling and sixpence. Dickens' memory served him well: with only one exception he repeated the verses exactly.

Langton reports from Mary Weller[35] that she and her sweetheart Thomas Gibson – a shipwright from the dockyard – would often romp with Charles in the fields near Fort Pitt. Dickens himself later wrote:

So, he played with that child, the whole day long, and they were very merry. The sky was so blue, the sun was so bright, the water was so sparkling, the leaves were so green, the flowers were so lovely, and they heard such singing-birds and saw so many butterflies, that everything was beautiful. This was in fine weather. When it rained, they loved to watch the falling drops, and to smell the fresh scents. When it blew, it was delightful to listen to the wind, and fancy what it said, as it came rushing from its home – where was that, they wondered! – whistling and howling, driving the clouds before it, bending the trees, rumbling in the chimneys, shaking the house, and making the sea roar in fury. But, when it snowed, that was best of all; for, they liked nothing so well as to look up at the white flakes falling fast and thick, like down from the breasts of millions of white birds; and to see how smooth and deep the drift was; and to listen to the hush upon the paths and roads.[36]

This sounds more like an adult romanticising about his childhood than a child appreciating his surroundings; but it is indicative of Dickens' remembrance of this period of his childhood as a happy experience. More realistically, the type of boyish knowledge gathered by a child such as he is given in another paper, and describes beautifully an atmosphere of Chatham:

There are some small out-of-the-way landing-places on the Thames and Medway where I do much of my summer idling. Running water is favourable to day-dreams, and a strong tidal river is the best of running water for mine. I like to watch the great ships standing out to sea or coming home richly laden, the active little steam-tugs confidently puffing with them to and from the sea-horizon, the fleet of barges that seem to have plucked their brown and russet sails from the ripe trees in the landscape, the heavy old colliers, light in ballast, floundering down before the tide, the light screw barks and schooners imperiously holding a straight course while the others patiently tack and go about, the yachts with their tiny hulls and great white sheets of canvas, the little sailing boats bobbing to and fro on their errands of pleasure or business, and – as is the nature of little people to do – making a prodigious fuss about their small affairs. Watching these objects, I still am under no obligation to think about them, or even so much as to see them, unless it perfectly suits my humour. As little am I obliged to hear the plash and flop of the tide, the ripple at my feet, the creaking windlass afar off, or the humming steamship paddles farther away yet. These, with the creaking little jetty on which I sit, and the gaunt high-water marks in the mud, and the broken causeway, and the broken stakes and piles leaning forward as if they were vain of their personal appearance, and looking for their reflexion in the water, will melt a train of fancy. Equally adaptable to any purpose or to none, are the pasturing sheep and kine upon the marshes, the gulls that wheel and dip around me, the crows (well out of gunshot) going home from the rich harvest-fields, the heron that has been out a-fishing and looks as melancholy, up there in the sky, as if it hadn't agreed with him. Everything within the range of the senses will, by the aid of the running water, lend itself to everything beyond that range, and work into a drowsy whole, not unlike a kind of tune, but for which there is no exact definition. One of these landing-places is near an old fort (I can see the Nore light from it with my pocket-glass), from which fort mysteriously emerges a boy, to whom I am much indebted for additions to my scanty stock of knowledge. He is a young boy, with an intelligent face burnt to a dust colour by the summer sun, and with crisp hair of the same hue. He is a boy in whom I have perceived nothing incompatible with habits of studious inquiry and meditation, unless an evanescent black eye (I was delicate of inquiring how occasioned) should be so considered. To him am I indebted for ability to identify a custom-house boat at any distance, and for acquaintance with all forms and ceremonies observed by a homeward-bound Indiaman coming up the river, when the custom-house officers go aboard her. But for him, I might never have heard of the 'dumb-ague', respecting which malady I am now learned. Had I never sat at his feet I might have finished my mortal career and never known that when I see a shire horse on a barge's sail that barge is a lime barge. For precious secrets in reference to beer am I likewise beholden to him, involving warning against the beer of a certain establishment, by reason of its having turned sour through failure in point of demand, though my young sage is not of opinion that similar deterioration has befallen the ale. He has also enlightened me touching the mushrooms of the marshes, and has gently reproved my ignorance in having supposed them to be impregnated with salt. His manner of imparting information is thoughtful, and appropriate to the scene. As he reclines beside me he pitches into the river a little stone or piece of grit, and then delivers himself oracularly, as though he spoke out of the centre of the spreading circle that it makes in the water. He never improves my mind without observing this formula. With the wise boy – whom I know by no other name than the Spirit of the Fort – I recently consorted on a breezy day when the river leaped about us and was full of life. I had seen the sheaved corn carrying in the golden fields as I came down to the river; and the rosey farmer, watching his labouring-men in the saddle on his cob, had told me how he had reaped his two hundred and sixty acres of long-strawed corn last week, and how a better week's work he had never done in all his days. Peace and abundance were on the countryside in beautiful forms and beautiful colours, and the harvest seemed even to be sailing out to grace the never reaped sea in the yellow-laden barges that mellowed the distance. It was on this occasion that the Spirit of the Fort, directing his remarks to a certain floating iron battery lately lying in that reach of the river, enriched my mind with his opinions on naval architecture, and informed me that he would like to be an engineer. I found him up to everything that is done in the contracting line by Messrs Peto and Brassey – cunning in the article of concrete – mellow in the matter of iron – great on the subject of gunnery. When he spoke of pile-driving and sluice-making he left me not a leg to stand on, and I can never sufficiently acknowledge his forbearance with me in my disabled state. While he thus discoursed he several times directed his eyes to one distant quarter of the landscape, and spoke with vague mysterious awe of 'the Yard'. Pondering his lessons after we had parted, I bethought me that the Yard was one of our large public dockyards, and that it lay hidden among the crops down in the dip behind the windmills, as if it modestly kept itself out of view in peaceful times, and sought to trouble no man.[37]

Whether the Spirit of the Fort was himself as a child – the adult Dickens meeting the child Dickens was a ploy he used elsewhere – or a childhood friend or, as it appears on the surface, a child he met as an adult, the atmosphere of the area immediately outside Chatham is captured in a manner impossible to find elsewhere. This clear fondness for the river and for boats was most likely reinforced by trips in an old-fashioned yacht called the *Chatham*, which belonged to the Navy Pay Office and was used by John Dickens to make trips to Sheerness.

The young Charles seemed easily to make friends with children of both sexes. Mary Weller recollected his constant companionship with Lucy Stroughill, a golden-haired little girl who lived next door,[38] and he committed to paper two birthday incidents involving childhood sweethearts:

I can very well remember being taken out to visit some peach-faced creature in a blue sash, and shoes to correspond, whose life I supposed to consist entirely of birthdays. Upon seed-cake, sweet wine, and shining presents, that glorified young person seemed to me to be exclusively reared. At so early a stage of my travels did I assist at the anniversary of her nativity (and became enamoured of her), that I had not yet acquired the recondite knowledge that a birthday is the common property of all who are born, but supposed it to be a special gift bestowed by the favouring heavens on that one distinguished infant. There was no other company, and we sat in a shady bower – under a table, as my better (or worse) knowledge leads me to believe – and were regaled with saccharine substances and liquids until it was time to part. A bitter powder was administered to me next morning, and I was wretched.[39]

Olympia was most beautiful (of course), and I loved her to that degree that I used to be obliged to get out of my little bed in the night, expressly to exclaim to Solitude, 'O, Olympia Squires!' . . . My memory presents a birthday when Olympia and I were taken by an unfeeling relative – some cruel uncle, or the like – to a slow torture called an Orrery. The terrible instrument was set up in the local theatre . . . It was a venerable and a shabby Orrery, at least one thousand stars and twenty-five comets behind the age. Nevertheless it was awful. When the low-spirited gentleman with the wand said 'Ladies and gentlemen' (meaning particularly Olympia and me), 'the lights are about to be put out, but there is not the slightest cause for alarm,' it was very alarming. Then the planets and stars began. Sometimes they wouldn't come on, sometimes they wouldn't go off, sometimes they had holes in them, and mostly they didn't seem to be good likenesses. All this time the gentleman with the wand was going on in the dark (tapping away at the Heavenly bodies between whiles, like a wearisome woodpecker), about a sphere revolving on its own axis eight hundred and ninety-seven thousand million of times – or miles – in two hundred and sixty-three thousand five hundred and twenty-four millions of something else, until I thought if this was a birthday it were better never to have been born. Olympia, also, became much depressed, and we both slumbered and woke cross, and still the gentleman was going on in the dark – whether up in the stars or down on the stage, it would have been hard to make out, if it had been worth trying – siphering away about planes of orbit, to such an infamous extent that Olympia, stung to madness, actually kicked me. A pretty spectacle when the lights were turned up again, and all the schools in the town (including the National, who had come in for nothing, and serve them right, for they were always throwing stones) were discovered with exhausted countenances, screwing their knuckles into their eyes, or clutching their heads of hair. A pretty birthday speech when Doctor Sleek, of the City-Free, bobbed up his powdered head in the stage-box, and said that before this assembly dispersed he really must beg to express his entire approval of a lecture as improving, as informing, as devoid of anything that could call a blush into the cheek of youth, as any it had been his lot to hear delivered. A pretty birthday altogether, when astronomy couldn't leave poor small Olympia Squires and me alone, but must put an end to our loves! For we never got over it; the threadbare Orrery outwore our mutual tenderness; the man with the wand was too much for the boy with the bow.[40]

Though this visit was not particularly successful – because of its subject content – generally speaking the theatre was a major attraction for the young Charles. He was taken to the Theatre Royal in Rochester, seeing Shakespeare's *Richard III* and *Macbeth*, William Barrymore's version of Pixerecourt's *Dog of Montargis*,

Rowe's *Tragedy of Jane Shore* and Lillo's *George Barnwell*.[41] He recollected the first visit he had made to a play more than thirty years later, in *Household Words*:

The first play! The promise; the hope deferred; the saving clause of 'no fine weather, no play' . . . Willingly did we submit, at five o'clock that evening, to the otherwise, and at any other time, detestable ordeal of washing, and combing, and being made straight. We did not complain when the soap got into our eyes; we bore the scraping of the comb, and the rasping of the brush without a murmur: we were going to the play, and we were happy. Dressed, of course, an hour too soon; drinking tea as a mere form and ceremony – for the tea might have been hay and hot water (not impossible), and the bread and butter might have been sawdust, for anything we could taste of it; sitting with petful impatience in the parlour, trying on the first pair of white kid gloves, making sure that the theatre would be burnt down, or that papa would never come home from the office, or mamma prevented, by some special interference of malignant demons, from having her dress fastened; or that (to a positive certainty) a tremendous storm of hail, rain, sleet, and thunder would burst out as we stepped into the cab, and send us, theatreless, to bed. We went to the play, and were happy. The sweet, dingy, shabby little country theatre, we declared, and believed, to be much larger than either Drury Lane or Covent Garden, of which little Master Cheesewright – whose father was a tailor, and always had orders – was wont to brag! Dear, narrow, uncomfortable, faded-cushioned, flea-haunted, single tier of boxes! The green curtain, with a hole in it, through which a bright eye peeped; the magnificent officers, in red and gold coats (it was a garrison town), in the stage-box, who volunteered, during the acts, the popular catch of –

> 'Ah! how, Sophia, can you leave
> Your lover, and of hope bereave?'

– for our special amusement and delectation, as we thought then, but, as we are inclined to fear now, under the influence of wine! The pit, with so few people in it; with the lady, who sold apples and oranges, sitting in a remote corner, like Pomona in the sulks. And the play when it did begin – stupid, badly acted, badly got up as it very likely was. Our intense, fear-stricken admiration of the heroine, when she let her back hair down, and went mad, in blue. The buff-boots of Digby the manager. The funny man (there never was such a funny man) in a red scratch wig who, when imprisoned in the deepest dungeon beneath the castle moat, sang a comic song about a leg of mutton. The sorry quadrille band in the orchestra, to our ears as scientifically melodious as though Costa had been conductor; Sivori, first fiddle; Richardson, flute; or Bottesini, double bass. The refreshment administered to us by kind hands during the intervals of performance, never to be forgotten – oranges, immemorial sponge-cakes. The admonitions to 'sit up', the warnings not to 'talk loud,' in defiance of which (seeing condonatory smiles on the faces of those we loved) we screamed outright with laughter, when the funny man, in the after-piece, essaying to scale a first floor front by means of a rope ladder, fell, ladder and all, to the ground. The final fall of the green curtain, followed by an aromatic perfume of orange-peel and lamp-oil, and the mysterious appearance of ghostly brown Holland draperies from the private boxes. Shawling, cloaking, home, and more primaries – for then it was when we for the first time 'sat up late,' and for the first time ever tasted sandwiches after midnight, or imbibed a sip, a very small sip, of hot something and water.[42]

There were visits, also, to the pantomime, described here as part of a fair that was visiting Chatham as part of its journey around the country:

The delights – the ten thousand million delights of a pantomime – come streaming upon us now – even of the pantomime which came lumbering down in Richardson's wagons[43] at fairtime to the dull little town in which we had the honour to be brought up,[44] and which a long row of small boys, with frills as white as they could be washed, and hands as clean as they would come were taken to behold the glories of, in fair daylight.
We feel again all the pride of standing in a body on the platform, the observed of all observers in the crowd below, while the junior usher pays away twenty-four ninepences to a stout gentleman under a Gothic arch, with a hoop of variegated lamps swinging over his head. Again we catch a glimpse (too

brief, alas!) of the lady with a green parasol in her hand, on the outside stage of the next show but one, who supports herself on one foot, on the back of a majestic horse, blotting-paper coloured and white; and once again our eyes open wide with wonder, and our hearts throb with emotion, as we deliver our cardboard check into the very hands of the Harlequin himself, who, all glittering with spangles, and dazzling with many colours, deigns to give us a word of encouragement and commendation as we pass into the booth!

. . . What mattered it that the stage was three yards wide, and four deep? *We* never saw it. We had no eyes, ears or corporeal senses, but for the pantomime.[45]

In 1819 and 1820 he was taken up to London to see the great clown Grimaldi in Christmas pantomimes, in whose honour he clapped his hands with great precocity.[46] His interest in the theatre, thus inspired, led him to arrange with his friends performances in the kitchen at Ordnance Terrace. Mary Weller reported: 'Sometimes Charles would come downstairs and say to me, "Now, Mary, clear the kitchen, we are going to have such a game," and then George Stroughill would come in with his Magic Lantern, and they would sing, recite, and perform parts of plays. Fanny and Charles often sang together at this time, Fanny accompanying on the pianoforte.'[47] Some of the plays performed were written by Charles himself: the introduction to the cheap edition of *Sketches by Boz* mentions 'certain tragedies achieved at the mature age of eight or ten, and represented with great applause to overflowing nurseries'.

It was while at Ordnance Terrace that Charles had his first experience of school, which he later recalled in *Household Words*:

We have faint recollections of a Preparatory Day-School, which we have sought in vain, and which must have been pulled down to make a new street, ages ago. We have dim impressions, scarcely amounting to a belief, that it was over a dyer's shop. We know that you went up steps to it; that you frequently grazed your knees in doing so; that you generally got your leg over the scraper, in trying to scrape the mud off a very unsteady little shoe. The mistress of the Establishment holds no place in our memory; but rampant on one eternal door-mat, in an eternal entry long and narrow, is a puffy pug-dog, with a

1. Crewe Hall, Cheshire. (National Monuments Record)

2a.   Mile End Terrace, Portsmouth. The bay-windowed house on the left is the one owned and lived in by William Pearce. John Dickens and his family lived next door. (Barbara Allen)

MILE END TERRACE.

FOR SALE, with immediate Possession, all that modern well built DWELLING-HOUSE, situate as above, late in the occupation of Mr. John Dickens. The House comprises, in the basement, a good kitchen and cellar; ground floor, two excellent parlours; first floor, two good bed chambers, and two garrets in the attic. The whole replete with fixtures. The Premises are 18 feet in width, and 120 feet in depth.

For further Particulars apply to Mr. WM. PEARCE, Mile End.

2b.   An entry from the *Hampshire Courier* for 22 and 29 June 1812, advertising the house at Mile End Terrace. It is interesting to note that William Pearce considered John Dickens' name worth mentioning in the advertisement. (British Library)

Rent due 25 Mar. 1812

Pearce	10.10 —
Harding	4 —
Creuze	13.13
Wadge	1.11.6
Ruvey	2.12.6
Walker	2.12.6
Price	2.12.6
Rackett	2.12.6
Cox	2.12.6
Stenson	2.12.6
Eyers	2.12.6
Bowyer	2.12.6
Chiverton	2.12.6
Marshall	2.12.6
Bidgood	3.0.3
Moses	3.0.3
Darcey	7.17.6
Good	5.5. —
Dickens	0.15 —
Smith	2 —
Harris	2 —
Clements	2 —
Kimber	2.10 —
Hall (Garden)	2.12.6

Rent due 24 June

Pearce	10.10 —
	5.19 —
Harding	13.13 —
Creuze	2.17 —
Ruvey	2.17 —
Walker	2.17 —
Price	2.17 —
Rackett	2.12.6
Cox	2.12.0
Stenson	2.17 —
Eyers	2.17 —
Bowyer	2.12.6
Chiverton	2.12.6
Marshall	3.12.9
Bidgood	3.12.9
Moses	7.17.6
Darcey	5.5. —
Good	0.15 —
Dickens	2 —
Smith	2 —
Harris	2 —
Clements	2.10 —
Kimber	2.12.6
Hall (Garden)	2.12.6

3. Pages from the rent book of William Pearce, held at the Dickens Birthplace Museum. The book shows the date the rent was due, the amount payable and the tenant. John Dickens appears on both pages. (Portsmouth City Museums)

4a. Hawke Street, Portsmouth, showing the Dickens home on the right-hand side, next to the lamp post. This photograph was taken in 1902. (Dickens House Museum)

56
Wish Street

1	Mr. Freman	&c	5	.	2 6
	Sarah Rear	Do	30	.	15 .
	Robt. Ford	Do	6	.	3 .
	Rd. Platt	Do	16	.	8 .
	Jas. Sheldwin	Do	14	.	7 .
	Tho. Hartley	Do	12	.	6 .
	Do. Store		2	.	1 .
	Hugh Bishop	Ho	20	.	10
	Major Williams	Do	20	.	10
39	Jno. Dicken	Do	20	.	10 .
38	Jno. Rout	Do	8	.	4 .
36	Jno. Hollis	Do	5	.	2 6

4b. A page from the Portsmouth Rate Books, showing John Dickens living at 39 Wish Street. (Portsmouth City Records Office)

5. A front view of Portsmouth dockyard, showing the Navy Pay Office where John Dickens worked: the first building on the right through the gates. First printed 1841. (British Library)

VALUABLE FREEHOLD ESTATES,
LAND TAX REDEEMED.
TO BE SOLD BY AUCTION,
By Mr. T. WILKINSON.

ON THURSDAY, April 10, 1817, at the MITRE Tavern, Chatham, between the hours of six and eight o'clock in the evening, (subject to such conditions as will be then and there produced.)

All that valuable brick built DWELLING HOUSE, with yard and garden, beautifully situated at Ordnance Place, fronting the road to Fort Pitt, commanding beautiful views of the surrounding country, and fit for the residence of a genteel family.

Together with all those four brick built DWELLING HOUSES, near the same, called Union Place, with five other Dwelling Houses, part fronting Fort Pitt-street, the whole of which are let to respectable tenants at will, and may be viewed any time previous to the Sale by leave of the Tenants, and Particulars known by application to the AUCTIONEER, St. Margaret's Bank, Rochester.

6a.   This advertisement appeared in the *Kentish Gazette* on 1, 4 and 8 April. John Dickens will have seen the advertisement and promptly taken the property, though to rent and not to buy: the name of the owner of the property was Baldock. It is interesting to note that the auction took place at the Mitre Tavern, which was later to feature in the social life of the Dickens family while they were at Chatham. (British Library)

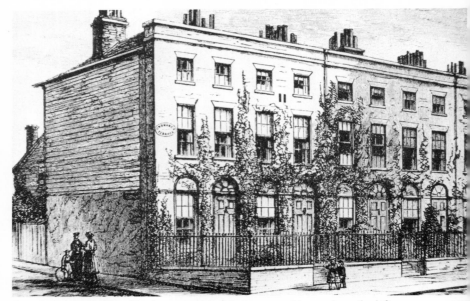

6b.   Ordnance Terrace, Chatham: number 2 is the second house from the left. (R. Langton, *The childhood and youth of Charles Dickens*)

7a. St Mary's Place, The Brook (*left*): the Dickens home was on the right, next to the chapel. (R. Langton, *The childhood and youth of Charles Dickens*)

7b. Giles' School, Best Street (*right*): the schoolroom was probably in a building behind the house, the roof of which can just be seen over the wall. (Dickens House Museum)

No.	Assessment.	OCCUPIER.	Sum charged.			Arrears brought forward to Lady Day, 1822.			Additions or Improvements.			RECEIVED.						No. of Summons	Decision of Ves Persons apply
												Amount.			No. of Receipt.	Folio in Cash Bk.			
			£.	s.	d.	£.	s.	d.	£.	s.	d.	£.	s.	d.					
16	22	Jno Dickens		18	4								9	2					empty
17	22	ally allort		18	4								18	4		42			

8a. An entry from the St Pancras Poor Rate book for 16 Bayham Street, covering the period April to September 1822. Note that only half the rate was paid, and that the house was empty at the end of the previous period. Taken together these points indicate that John Dickens was in occupancy from 25 June. (London Borough of Camden)

8b. Wellington House Academy. (R. Langton, *The childhood and youth of Charles Dickens*)

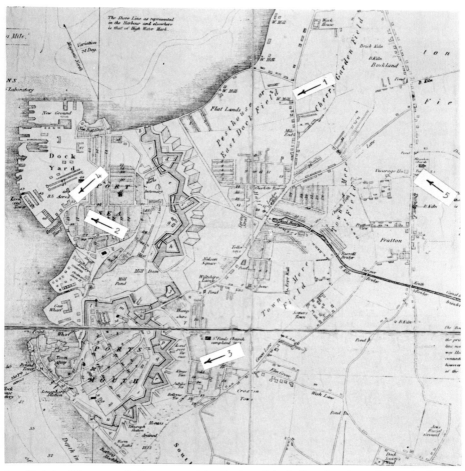

9. *Sketch of Portsmouth, Portsea, and the Dockyard, including also the various suburbs and the SW part of Portsea Island, 1823.* Reproduced by the City Engineer for the *Hampshire Telegraph and Post*, 27 December 1929. The map shows: 1. Mile End Terrace, 2. Hawke Street, 3. Wish Street, 4. Navy Pay Office, 5. Kingston Church. (Portsmouth Central Library)

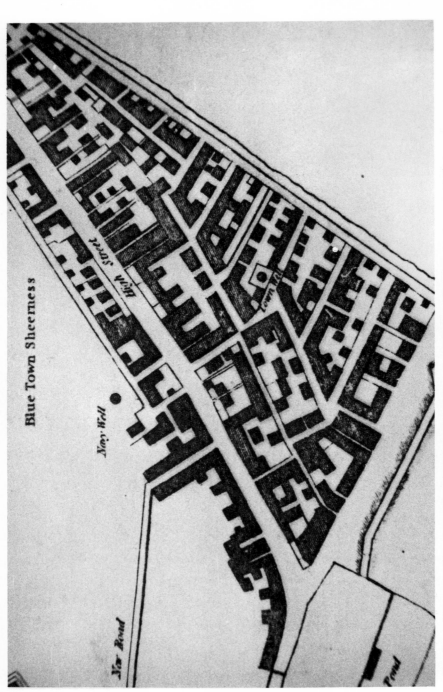

10. Blue Town, Sheerness. The exact site of the Dickens' home has not been discovered, but the theatre which it stood next to was on a corner on the north side of the High Street. All the buildings on that side of the High Street were demolished between 1817 and 1821 and the area enclosed within a dockyard wall. The map was drawn by R. Dodd in 1800. (Public Record Office)

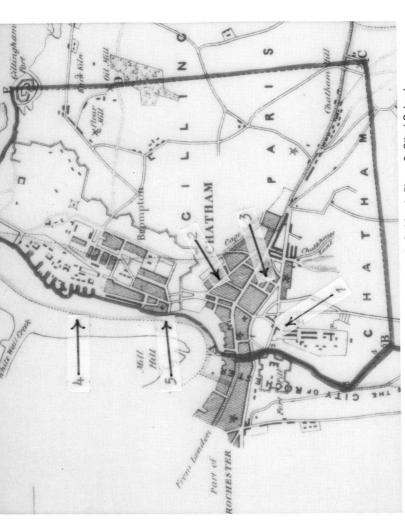

11. Map of Chatham, showing: 1. Ordnance Terrace, 2. St Mary's Place, 3. Giles' School,
4. Chatham Dockyard, 5. St Mary's Church. It is particularly interesting to note how few houses
there are in Ordnance Terrace and the road leading to Fort Pitt, and to relate this to the
advertisement in Plate 6. The map is taken from *Plans of the Cities and Boroughs of England and
Wales* . . . by Robert K. Dawson, published in 1832. (British Library)

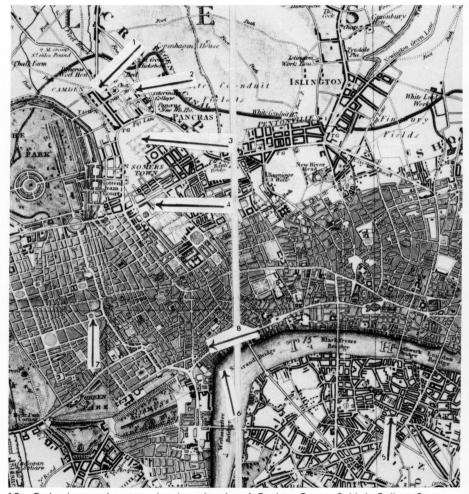

12. Early nineteenth-century London, showing: 1. Bayham Street, 2. Little College Street, 3. Johnson Street, 4. Gower Street North, 5. Lant Street, 6. Hungerford Stairs, 7. Royal Academy of Music, 8. Chandos Street. From *A new topographical map of the country* . . . (British Library MAP 78/2650, ref. no. 3479(29))

13. Hungerford Stairs, showing the blacking warehouse to the right of the stairs. Charles Dickens would have worked at the bow window overlooking the river. (Greater London Record Office)

14.   Dickens at the blacking warehouse, by Fred Barnard.

15. John Dickens, etched by Samuel Hayden from a bust. (Dickens House Museum)

16. No. 1 Lant Street, Borough. The entrance to the house was through the door with the round archway. The house covered a large site and was later altered to form two houses, the nearer door then being added. The entrance to the woodyard mentioned by Dickens was through the gateway. (London Borough of Southwark)

17a.   No. 29 Johnson Street, from an article 'In Somers Town' by W. Pett Ridge.

28	20	Horace Parker	16	8
29	20	Caroline Dickens Weldon	16	8
30	20	Burton	16	8

17b.   Entry for 29 Johnson Street from the St Pancras Poor Rate book for January 1825. Notice the confusion over names. (London Borough of Camden)

18. Chandos Street, Covent Garden. Warren's Blacking moved to the second shop on the left. Dickens wrote of wearing the stones smooth by going backwards and forwards to the public house opposite. From a watercolour by T. C. Dibdin, 1851. (City of Westminster)

19.   Elizabeth Dickens, by John W. Gilbert. (Dickens House Museum)

20.   Portrait said to be of Charles Dickens as a boy. (Dickens House Museum)

personal animosity towards us, who triumphs over Time. The bark of that baleful Pug, a certain radiating way he had of snapping at our undefended legs, the ghastly grinning of his moist black muzzle and white teeth, and the insolence of his crisp tail curled like a pastoral crook, all live and flourish. From an otherwise unaccountable association of him with a fiddle, we conclude that he was of French extraction, and his name *Fidèle*. He belonged to some female, chiefly inhabiting a back parlor, whose life appears to us to have been consumed in sniffing, and in wearing a brown beaver bonnet. For her, he would sit up and balance cake upon his nose, and not eat it until twenty had been counted. To the best of our belief, we were once called in to witness this performance; when, unable, even in his milder moments, to endure our presence, he instantly made at us, cake and all.[48]

Though the Dickens family's home was strictly speaking in Chatham, it was considered that they were residents of Rochester just as much as Chatham, there being no obvious borderline between the two. In his article *Dullborough Town* Dickens brought together both places under the same name. It was, however, Rochester that he had in mind when he wrote the following:

Of course the town had shrunk fearfully, since I was a child there. I had entertained the impression that the High-street was at least as wide as Regent-street, London, or the Italian Boulevard at Paris. I found it little better than a lane. There was a public clock in it, which I had supposed to be the finest clock in the world; whereas it now turned out to be as inexpressive, moon-faced, and weak a clock as ever I saw. It belonged to a Town Hall, where I had seen an Indian (who I now suppose wasn't an Indian) swallow a sword (which I now suppose he didn't). This edifice had appeared to me in those days so glorious a structure, that I had set it up in my mind as the model on which the Genie of the Lamp built the palace for Aladdin. A mean little brick heap, like a demented chapel, with a few yawning persons in leather gaiters, and in the last extremity for something to do, lounging at the door with their hands in their pockets, and calling themselves a Corn Exchange![49]

SOME NEIGHBOURS AT ORDNANCE TERRACE

Next door to the Dickens home, at the first house in the terrace, from about 1819 lived the Stroughill family, which included George, a somewhat older boy and Charles' greatest friend at this . time, and his sister Lucy, a constant companion of Charles.[50] Their father was William Stroughill, a plumber and glazier, who moved out of the terrace at about the same time as John Dickens and soon afterwards built some houses in the same road.[51]

For a clear picture of the other neighbours, and of the style of life which the Dickens family enjoyed, it is necessary to turn to their famous son's later writings. One of the most interesting pieces appeared in *Sketches by Boz* and described a neighbour called simply 'the old lady'. She was almost certainly Mary Ellen Newnham, who lived at the fourth house in Ordnance Terrace, and the sketch, which first appeared in print in 1835, seems to have been written after a return visit to the town by Dickens some time after the death of the old lady's husband, Richard Newnham, who died on 12 June 1827 at the age of 76.

In the sketch he describes the terrace as 'a neat row of houses in the most airy and pleasant part' of the parish, and the old lady's house itself as 'a perfect picture of quiet neatness', with a beeswaxed table, precisely arranged nicknacks, a royal portrait and two old-fashioned watches; the old lady engages her day in needlework and bible-reading; she sees little company except for little girls who live in the terrace and who visit on regular days to drink tea with her. Adult visitors, when they are received, are plied with sherry. She occasionally visits her neighbours in the terrace and is scrupulous in returning their visits, which occasions are ceremoniously genteel. She is generously benevolent to the old, the poor and the church, and she has a maid to look after her.

The connections between the Dickens and the Newnham families are most interesting. The Newnhams lived at their house in the terrace throughout the Dickens family's stay, and a strong friendship developed between them. Richard Newnham – a retired tailor – was in a very comfortable position: besides owning his home at Chatham he also owned another at Southwark and had several thousand pounds invested at the Bank of England. It seems that because of his sound financial situation he was able to loan money to John Dickens, since in 1824, when John Dickens –

back in London – was declared bankrupt, he was appointed Assignee of the Dickens estate and effects. However, he declined to act, and the relationship between the two remained cordial.

When Richard Newnham died in 1827 he left in his will to John Dickens' daughter, Letitia, a sixth share in the dividends of a £300 trust, to be realised on her marriage or coming of age. Later that same year John Dickens, in remembrance of his neighbour, bestowed upon his last child, born that year, the name Augustus Newnham Dickens. The old lady lived on and the connections were kept up, as can be gathered from the presumed visit of Charles prior to the writing of the sketch. In March 1836, when Dickens was planning his honeymoon, he wrote to Catherine Hogarth, his bride-to-be: 'it strikes me, the best plan would be, when we are married, for us to go straight to Rochester. Mother can write to the "Old Lady's" servant; and she, I have no doubt will procure us comfortable lodgings there.'[52] When Mrs Newnham died in 1843 she left some money and possessions in her will to both Fanny and Letitia.[53]

Another neighbour later described by Dickens is the 'half-pay Captain', the title of a sketch which first appeared in print together with 'the old lady'. He is an uproarious retired naval officer, who exhibits bluff and unceremonious behaviour. He sits in the front garden overlooking the Medway and the dockyard, smoking cigars and demanding ale from the old lady. He believes he knows how to fix all kinds of odd jobs, yet somehow manages to be more of a nuisance than a help.

But all this is nothing to his seditious conduct in public life. He attends every vestry meeting that is held: always opposes the constituted authorities of the parish, denounces the profligacy of the churchwardens, contests legal points against the vestry-clerk, *will* make the tax-gatherer call for his money till he won't call any longer, and then sends it; finds fault with the sermon every Sunday, says that the organist ought to be ashamed of himself, offers to back himself for any amount to sing psalms better than all the children put together, male and female; and, in short, conducts himself in the most turbulent and uproarious manner. The worst of it, that having a high regard for the old lady, he wants to make her a convert to his views, and therefore walks into her little parlour with his newspaper in his hand, and talks violent politics by the hour. He is a charitable, open-hearted old fellow at bottom, after all, so, although he puts the old lady a little out occasionally, they agree very well in the main, and she laughs as much at each feat of his handiwork when it is all over, as anybody else.[54]

The half-pay Captain was probably Duncan Calder, who lived at the third house in the terrace. His cantankerous behaviour towards the parish authorities seems a likely cause for the reduction in the ratable value of first his home and then the other houses in the terrace, as recorded in the rate books.

ELIZABETH DICKENS

References to Elizabeth Dickens at this time are few and far between, but a perceptive description of her from some years later seems applicable here:

Mrs Dickens was a little woman, who had been very nice-looking in her youth. She had very bright hazel eyes, and was as thoroughly good-natured, easy-going, companionable a body as one would wish to meet with. The likeness between her and Mrs. Nickleby is simply the exaggeration of some slight peculiarities. She possessed an extraordinary sense of the ludicrous, and her power of imitation was something quite astonishing. On entering a room she almost unconsciously took an inventory of its contents, and if anything happened to strike her as out of place or ridiculous, she would afterwards describe it in the quaintest possible manner. In like manner she noted personal peculiarities of her friends and acquaintances. She had also a fine vein of pathos, and could bring tears to the eyes of her listeners when narrating some sad event . . . I am of opinion that a great deal of Dickens's genius was inherited from his mother. He possessed from her a keen appreciation of the droll and of the pathetic, as also considerable dramatic talent. Mrs. Dickens has often sent my sisters and myself into uncontrollable fits of laughter by her funny sayings and inimitable mimicry. Charles was decidedly fond of her . . .[55]

JOHN DICKENS AT CHATHAM

There can be little doubt that John Dickens enjoyed a very good salary during the six years he spent at Chatham. Back in London, during 1815 and 1816, he was receiving £200 a year; but because of Outport Allowances this was increased immediately on departure for Sheerness by about £91 a year. Then, in 1820, having completed fifteen years' service with the Navy Pay Office, his basic salary rose to £350 a year, making a total income of £441. It had therefore, in a period of five years, increased by 120 per cent. Throughout his years at Chatham he worked in the Pay Office building and continued to rise in the office hierarchy: in 1821 he was listed as 3rd Clerk at Chatham, and following reorganisation in December 1821 he was transferred from the Pay Branch to the Branch for Inspecting Seamen's Wills and Powers of Attorney and controlling Licensed Agents.[56]

Socially he believed in enjoying himself: there were many parties and social gatherings, including entertainments at the Mitre – the famous inn at Chatham where both Nelson and the Duke of Clarence (later to become William IV) had stayed. There were trips to the local theatre as well as the occasional jaunt to the theatre in London. He enjoyed books, he enjoyed walking with his son, he enjoyed taking his children to Sheerness on the Navy Pay Yacht; he had a fine new house, a large family and two servants. Taken together – his income, his work, his house, his neighbours, his entertainments, his servants – these all indicate a firm middle-class background. Yet his very style of living was a precarious one, and not unusually so, as this extract from R. G. Hobbes' autobiography clearly illustrates:

We must return for a moment to the Civil Service. The salaries of the Dockyard Officers and clerks were at that time paid quarterly, and often we – I mean my own household – were brought to extremities before salary day. We were obliged to run up little tradesmen's bills, and when these were paid but a small sum was left to go on with. The case was doubtless the same with all the married junior clerks. A debt, moreover, had been incurred by me for unavoidable family expenses, and that had to be paid by quarterly installments. I could not well have got through that trying period but for the help of kind friends whom Providence raised up, and whose generosity I can never forget.[57]

No doubt John Dickens too ran up tradesmen's bills and turned to friends: he had a house to furnish and run, a growing family to clothe, feed and care for, servants to keep, entertainments to stage and attend, and a position in the community to keep up.

There are two incidents which, though small in themselves, illustrate well the manner in which he approached life. First, in his need to identify with the community in which he now lived and to show his standing as a man of books, he subscribed in 1817 to a local publication, *The history and antiquities of Rochester and its environs;*[58] there, proudly printed at the beginning of the book, is John Dickens' name, listed as a subscriber. This was of course just one of many books and periodicals that the pay clerk bought, but it was special since he knew that other readers would identify him with it. The second incident concerned a very serious fire which tore through Chatham on 3 March 1820. It started in a bakehouse in the High Street and eventually destroyed 53 houses and 13 warehouses.[59] John Dickens was there, taking careful note of the facts, since an account reported to have been written by him[60] appeared in both the *Kentish Gazette* – a local paper – and no less a newspaper than *The Times!*[61] Afterwards he was selected to sit on a vestry committee to help relieve those who had suffered loss in the fire, the committee being no doubt impressed by his journalistic achievement. They may have been impressed, too, if it was he who persuaded all his neighbours to subscribe to the fund: John Dickens himself donated two guineas, as did Richard Newnham; his ex-neighbour Mrs Watherstone could afford only one guinea, and Mrs Calder just five shillings.[62]

Through these two incidents shine aspects of the sort of person John Dickens wished to be: a man of books, a writer, a generous man, a man who wished to identify with and give his time to the local community. He might less generously have been labelled a status-seeker. But whatever the status he sought, or however he organised – or failed to organise – his income, his approach to life was financially unrealistic. On 14 August 1819 he borrowed £200 from a James Milbourne of Kennington Green, Surrey, to be paid back at £26 per annum for the rest of his life.[63] It is interesting to ponder on the reason for this loan, which in 1987 would be worth about £4700: was it to settle a number of smaller bills, or to finance some expansive scheme? At some time he also borrowed money from his neighbour Richard Newnham. His response to both loans was neither gentlemanly nor neighbourly. The annual payment to James Milbourne was not kept up, forcing the creditor to resort to calling on John Dickens' brother-in-law, Thomas Culliford Barrow, who had countersigned the agreement; the debt was cancelled by Barrow on 26 May 1821 by payment of £213, and the papers relating to the affair were still in the possession of Barrow when he died in 1857, the debt never having been settled.[64] The debt to Richard Newnham was still outstanding as late as December 1824.[65]

There was a family argument over the debt cancelled by Thomas Barrow, and this must have given John Dickens cause to reconsider his residential situation: perhaps, even, Thomas Barrow demanded such reconsideration, for a move was made away from Ordnance Terrace just one month before the debt was settled. But care must be taken on this point: it is true that the house into which the Dickens family moved was smaller than Ordnance Terrace, and it certainly did not look as attractive; but the area in which it was situated was at that time certainly not inferior, being the residential district for most of those officers who worked in the dockyard yet did not qualify for a residence there. The saving in rent would have proved a very small part of his income, which was then at its peak. Why then was the move made? There are a number of possibilities: to save money, either on his own initiative or with the prompting of Thomas Barrow; on demand from his landlord, if he was neglecting to pay his rent, as he was neglecting to pay his debts; and in anticipation of the marriage of Mary Allen, which was to occur later that year and would thus reduce the size of the household and the amount of money coming into the house. Whatever the reason, the move was not a progressive step and would have been made out of necessity rather than choice.

The Dickens' home at Ordnance Terrace still stands and is privately owned. The future of the house has been in jeopardy for some years, and its condition has gradually deteriorated. Nevertheless, the Rochester branch of the Dickens Fellowship has fought hard against moves to demolish the building, and more recently the Medway Borough Council has put a preservation order on the property and has considered its purchase and restoration. The building is marked with a plaque.

18 ST MARY'S PLACE, THE BROOK

Forster was the first person to write of Charles Dickens' next home: 'the house where he lived in Chatham, which had a plain-looking whitewashed plaster-front and a small garden before and behind, was in St. Mary's-place, otherwise called the Brook, and next door to a Baptist meeting-house called Providence-chapel, of which a Mr. Giles to be presently mentioned was minister'.[66]

There is only circumstantial evidence to fix the length of stay at The Brook with any accuracy. The rate books for Ordnance Terrace indicate that John Dickens left that address after May 1821, and he does not appear again anywhere in the rate books for the Chatham area. His next appearance in the rate books can be found in Camden Town, London, where he paid the rates from the end of June 1822. The length of stay at The Brook must have been, therefore, just one year.

It is possible that the house in St Mary's Place was brought to the attention of John Dickens by William Giles, Charles' schoolmaster, since Giles' sister later clearly remembered the house at Ordnance Terrace, and so it would seem that Charles started attending Giles' school before leaving Ordnance Terrace. That St Mary's Place was directly next door to the Chapel of Giles' father seems more than coincidence. The house, first given specifically as number 18 by Langton, was semi-detached, and with six rooms[67] could not have been much smaller than Ordnance Terrace; but just as the first Dickens home in Chatham must have been crowded, so too must their new home have been. Though it was not so crowded that there was not some spare room: in his fragment of autobiography Dickens later wrote: 'My father had left a small collection of books in a little room upstairs to which I had access (for it adjoined my own), and which nobody else in our house ever troubled.'[68] There were probably five children, three adults and Mary Weller and Jane Bonny to squeeze into the little house. There is difficulty in stating the exact number of children at this stage, because of a lack of information concerning the death of Harriet Ellen Dickens. She was born on 3 September 1819 and Mary Weller recollected that she died before the family left Chatham;[69] Gladys Storey, however, says that she died in London, of smallpox.[70]

Nevertheless, the structure of the household did change not long after the move. On 11 December 1821 Mary Allen married

Thomas Lamert (pronounced Lammer), an army surgeon in Chatham, and they soon after moved to Ireland, taking with them Jane Bonny. The marriage took place in St Mary's church, Chatham, and was witnessed by John and Elizabeth Dickens. Thomas Lamert, for whom this was a second marriage, had been courting Mary Allen for some time, and his stepson James Lamert had become a favourite with Charles, greatly encouraging his interest in the theatre. When the move to Ireland for the newly-weds arrived James Lamert stayed behind to live with the Dickens family.

Not long afterwards, on 11 March 1822, yet another child was born to the Dickenses and was given the same name as the child who had died in Portsmouth, Alfred. He was baptised at St Mary's, Chatham, on 3 April 1822 and just as the earlier child had been given Aunt Fanny's surname as a second name – Alfred Allen Dickens – so was the new baby given her new surname – Alfred Lamert Dickens. Indeed Aunt Fanny must have been a dearly loved and close member of the family – assisting in the children's upbringing, helping to pay some of the family bills out of her £50 a year pension and bestowing kindnesses on her nephews and nieces. A brief glimpse of her role is given in a few lines from one of Dickens' later writings, when he is writing of being taken to the orrery: 'I had expressed a profane wish in the morning that it was a play: for which a serious aunt had probed my conscience deep, and my pocket deeper, by reclaiming a bestowed half-crown'.[71] It must have come as a profound shock when news came from Ireland within a year of her marriage that she had died. She was aged only 34, and was buried at Cork on 25 September 1822. The Dickens family's connections with the Lamert family were, two years later, to administer a second profound shock to young Charles, when they were to introduce him to work in the blacking warehouse.

According to Mary Weller life at The Brook was not so lively as it had been at Ordnance Terrace,[72] though she may well have been referring to life for the adults rather than the children. For them the usual world of childish pursuits continued much as before:

It was on a New Year's Day that I fought a duel. Furious with love and jealousy, I 'went out' with another gentleman of honor, to assert my passion for the loveliest and falsest of her sex. I estimate the age of that young lady to have been about nine – my own age, about ten. I knew the Queen of my soul, as 'the youngest Miss Clickitt but one.' I had offered marriage, and my proposals had been very favorably received, though not definitively closed with. At which juncture, my enemy – Paynter, by name – arose out of some abyss or cavern, and came between us. The appearance of the Fiend Paynter, in the Clickitt Paradise, was altogether so mysterious and sudden, that I don't know where he came from; I only know that I found him, on the surface of this earth, one afternoon late in the month of December, playing at hot boiled beans and butter with the youngest Miss Clickitt but one. His conduct on that occasion was such, that I sent a friend to Paynter. After endeavouring with levity to evade the question, by pulling the friend's cap off and throwing it into a cabbage-garden, Paynter referred my messenger to his cousin – a goggle-eyed Being worthy of himself. Preliminaries were arranged, and by my own express stipulation the meeting was appointed for New Year's Day, in order that one of us might quit this state of existence on a day of mark. I passed a considerable portion of the last evening of the old year in arranging my affairs. I addressed a pathetic letter, and a goldfinch, to the youngest Miss Clickitt but one (to be delivered into her own hands by my friend, in case I should fall), and I wrote another letter for my mother, and made a disposition of my property: which consisted of books, some coloured engravings of Bamfylde Moore Carew, Mrs. Shipton, and others, in a florid style of art, and a rather choice collection of marbles. While engaged in these last duties, I suffered the keenest anguish, and wept abundantly. The combat was to begin with fists, but was to end any how. Dark presentiments overshadowed my mind, because I had heard, on reliable authority, that Paynter (whose father was pay-master of some regiment stationed in the sea-port where the conflict impended), had a dirk and meant the worst. I had no other arms, myself, than a blank cartridge, of which ammunition we used to get driblets from the soldiers when they practised, by following them up with tobacco, and bribing them with pipes-full screwed in old copies, to pretend to load and not to do it. This cartridge my friend and second had specially recommended me, on the combat's assuming a mortal appearance, to explode on the fell Paynter: which I, with some

indefinite view of blowing that gentleman up, had undertaken
to do, though the engineering details of the operation were not
at all adjusted. We met in a sequestered trench, among the
fortifications. Paynter had access to some old military stores,
and appeared on the ground in the regulation-cap of a full-
grown Private of the Second Royal Veteran Battalion. – I see the
boy now, coming from among the stinging-nettles in an angle
of the trench, and making my blood run cold by his terrible
appearance. Preliminaries were arranged, and we were to begin
the struggle – this again was my express stipulation – on the
word being given, 'The youngest Miss Clickitt but one!' At this
crisis, a difference of opinion arose between the seconds,
touching the exact construction of that article in the code of
honor which prohibits 'hitting below the waistcoat;' and I rather
think it arose from *my* second's having manoeuvred the whole
of *my* waistcoat into the neighbourhood of my chin. However it
arose, expressions were used which Paynter, who I found had
a very delicate sense of honor, could not permit to pass. He
immediately dropped his guard, and appealed to me whether it
was not our duty most reluctantly to forego our own gratification
until the two gentlemen in attendance on us had established
their honor? I warmly assented; I did more; I immediately took
my friend aside, and lent him the cartridge. But, so unworthy
of our confidence were those seconds that they declined,
in spite alike of our encouragements and our indignant
remonstrances to engage. This made it plain both to Paynter
and myself, that we had but one painful course to take; which
was, to leave them ('with loathing,' Paynter said, and I highly
approved), and go away arm in arm. He gave me to understand
as we went along that he too was a victim of the perfidy of the
youngest Miss Clickitt but one, and I became exceedingly fond
of him before we parted.[73]

For Charles, school, which he attended with his sister Fanny,
was a most important part of his life. He had attended a first
school in Rome Lane, already mentioned, but a greater influence
seems to have been exerted by the master at his second school,
William Giles.[74] Giles, the son of the minister of the chapel next
door to the house on The Brook, was about 23 years old and not
long down from Oxford when he first taught Charles. He had two
younger brothers, John and Samuel, both just a little older than

Charles, and a sister five years his senior who later remembered the relationship between Charles and his schoolmaster.[75] Charles was often in the company of the Giles family, particularly young Samuel, who was almost his daily companion,[76] and Dickens, talking of John Giles, later recalled the time 'when they were no strangers to each other, when they rambled together through the same Kentish fields, and mingled in the same sports'.[77] The schoolmaster and his sister were struck with Charles' bright appearance, unusual intelligence and good manners, and William Giles gave him every encouragement in his education, an extra effort that soon produced positive results. Miss Giles remembered Charles as a very handsome boy with long curly hair of a light colour and a very amiable, agreeable disposition.[78] He was quite at home at all sorts of parties and thoroughly enjoyed himself at fifth of November celebrations. He and his friends enjoyed themselves also by pretending to talk a foreign language around the streets, to impress passers-by, a game that he took with him to a later school in London.

Giles' school was situated at the corner of Rhode Street and Best Street, a short walk from The Brook, a walk Charles must have made many times, proudly displaying the white beaver hat that pupils at the school were expected to wear. He later wore the same hat on his journey from Chatham to London and even later was still wearing it when, during his father's imprisonment, he was summoned before an official to have the family's possessions valued. Charles always remembered his schoolmaster with affection, responding no doubt to the teacher's recognition of his abilities. Forster later wrote: 'when, about halfway through the publication of *Pickwick*, his old teacher sent a silver snuff-box with inscription to "the inimitable Boz", it reminded him of praise far more precious obtained by him at his first year's examination in the Clover-lane[79] academy, when his recitation of a piece out of the *Humourist's Miscellany* about Doctor Bolus, had received, unless his youthful vanity bewildered him, a double encore'.[80]

William Giles was well known as a cultivated reader and elocutionist, and undoubtedly had a great influence on Charles at this very formative period of the child's education. But there were other influences at work, too: the vivid world of the imagination, as Forster indicates:

Of the 'readings' and 'imaginations' which he describes as

brought away from Chatham, this authority can tell us. It is one of the many passages in *Copperfield* which are literally true, and its proper place is here. 'My father had left a small collection of books in a little room upstairs to which I had access (for it adjoined my own), and which nobody else in our house ever troubled. From that blessed little room, *Roderick Random*, *Peregrine Pickle*, *Humphrey Clinker*, *Tom Jones*, the *Vicar of Wakefield*, *Don Quixote*, *Gil Blas*, and *Robinson Crusoe* came out, a glorious host, to keep me company. They kept alive my fancy, and hope of something beyond that place and time, – they, and the *Arabian Nights*, and the *Tales of Genii*, – and did me no harm; for, whatever harm was in them, was not there for me; *I* knew nothing of it. It is astonishing to me now, how I found time, in the midst of my porings and blunderings over heavier themes, to read those books I did. It is curious to me how I could ever have consoled myself under my small troubles (which were great troubles to me), by impersonating my favourite characters in them . . . I have been Tom Jones (a child's Tom Jones, a harmless creature) for a week together. I have sustained my own idea of Roderick Random for a month at a stretch, I verily believe. I had a greedy relish for a few volumes of voyages and travels – I forget what, now, – that were on those shelves; and for days and days I can remember to have gone about my region of our house, armed with the centre-piece out of an old set of boot-trees; the perfect realisation of Captain Somebody, of the royal British navy, in danger of being beset by savages, and resolved to sell his life at a great price . . . When I think of it, the picture always rises in my mind, of a summer evening, the boys at play in the churchyard, and I sitting on my bed, reading as if for life. Every barn in the neighbourhood, every stone in the church, and every foot of the churchyard, had some association of its own, and stood for some locality made famous in them. I have seen Tom Pipes go climbing the church-steeple; I have watched Strap, with the knapsack on his back, stopping to rest himself upon the wicket-gate; and I *know* that Commodore Trunnion held that club with Mr. Pickle, in the parlor of our little village alehouse.' Every word of this personal recollection had been written down as fact, some years before it found its way into *David Copperfield*: the only change in the fiction being his omission of the name of a cheap series of novelists then in the course of publication, by which his father had become happily the owner of so large a lump of literary treasure in his small collection of books.[81]

Besides this collection of books the little attic on The Brook also contained *The Spectator*, Johnson's *Idler*, Goldsmith's *Citizen of the world* and Mrs Inchbald's *Collection of Farces*. The cheap series of novelists mentioned by Forster probably contained Walpole's *Castle of Otranto*, Johnson's *Rasselas*, Voltaire's *Candide*, Fielding's *Jonathan Wild* and *Amelia*, Lesage's *Devil on two sticks*, and Richardson's *Pamela*.[82] Washington Irving's books were also well read, as Dickens enthusiastically wrote to him in a letter in 1841.[83]

Mary Weller also recalled Charles retiring to the top room of the house at The Brook, spending what should have been his play hours in poring over his books or acting to the furniture in the room. She said that it was 'his custom to sit with his book in his left hand, and constantly moving it up and down, and at the same time sucking his tongue'.[84] In turn, Charles developed a talent for telling stories himself and even managed to write a tragedy, which he called *Misnar, the sultan of India*.[85]

But a more real tragedy was soon to befall the imaginative little boy, as indeed it was to engulf the whole Dickens family. In the summer of 1822 John Dickens was recalled to work at Somerset House in London. Most of the family's goods were packed up and sent to London by boat. Some were sold, the parlour chairs for example going to Thomas Gibson, who, soon after the family left, married Mary Weller.[86] In place of Mary Weller the family took with them to London a small servant girl from the Chatham workhouse. And then, almost at the last minute it seemed, Charles was asked to stay behind with Mr Giles for a little longer.

It is impossible to say how long he remained with his schoolmaster in the large house at the corner of Rhode Street and Best Street, but it could not have been for long. An estimate of three months should be considered: the evidence points to the Dickens family residing at Camden Town near London from 25 June 1822, and this should be compared with a later piece of writing by Dickens that has been offered in the past as descriptive of *his* arrival at Camden Town: 'I was taken home, and there was Debt at home as well as Death';[87] if this were so, then the death could well have been that of Mary Lamert, his Aunt Fanny, which occurred in September 1822. The period spent in the Giles' home does not seem to have been outstanding in Charles' mind, since nowhere does he mention it. Giles' sister describes it as 'some little time'.[88] But if Charles did not recollect this short stay away from his family, he did remember his eventual departure from Chatham. 'On the night before we came away,' he told Forster, 'my good master came flitting in among the packing-cases to give me Goldsmith's *Bee* as a keepsake. Which I kept for his sake, and its own, a long time afterwards.'[89]

He remembered the coach office, too, though it was Simpson's and not Timpson's: 'When I departed from Dullborough [Chatham] in the strawy arms of Timpson's Blue-Eyed Maid, Timpson's was a moderate-sized coach-office (in fact, a little coach-office), with an oval transparency in the window, which looked beautiful by night, representing one of Timpson's coaches in the act of passing a mile-stone on the London road with great velocity, completely full inside and out, and all the passengers dressed in the first style of fashion, and enjoying themselves tremendously.'[90] The reality, however, was not quite as exciting as the coach-office would have him believe: 'Through all the years that have since passed have I ever lost the smell of the damp straw in which I was packed – like game – and forwarded, carriage paid, to the Cross Keys, Wood Street, Cheapside, London? There was no other inside passenger, and I consumed my sandwiches in solitude and dreariness, and it rained hard all the way, and I thought life sloppier than I had expected to find it.'[91]

Number 18 St Mary's Place deteriorated badly during the early part of this century and then suffered bomb damage during the second world war. It was left derelict for some time and finally demolished in the 1950s. William Giles' house survived a little longer, being pulled down in the 1960s. The sites of both houses are now covered by car parks. A nearby block of flats has been named Copperfield House.

The years from five to eleven had been good ones for Charles. Forster described the Chatham area as the birthplace of Charles Dickens' fancy,[92] and so it was. Dickens himself wrote: 'We received our earliest and most enduring impressions among barracks and soldiers, and ships and sailors. We have outgrown no story of voyage and travel, no love of adventure, no ardent interest in voyagers and travellers.'[93] On many occasions, in his own writings, he turned to the area to let his imagination once again explore the countryside, the towns and the villages, as it had done when he was a child. And when in 1857 he had the opportunity to buy a house in the area – Gads Hill Place – he jumped at it, and lived the last thirteen years of his life there. But that house had a very special attraction for him: at the time he was buying it he wrote to Angela Burdett-Coutts: 'I used to look at it as a wonderful Mansion (which God knows it is not), when I was a very odd little child with the faint shadows of all my books in my head'.[94] And even more than that it was associated with the childhood ambitions inspired by his father, as Forster described:

> Often we had travelled past it together, years and years before it became his home; and never without some allusion to what he told me when first I saw it in his company, that amid his recollections connected with his childhood it held always a prominent place, for, upon first seeing it as he came from Chatham with his father, and looking up at it with much admiration, he had promised that he might himself live in it, when he came to be a man, if he would only work hard enough. Which for a long time was his ambition.[95]

4

London, from Camden Town to the Marshalsea

Though past biographers have shown some confusion over the date that John Dickens brought his family and his young son from Chatham to London, examination of available documents makes it clear that the Navy Pay Office moved their clerk to the capital in June 1822. There he rejoined two colleagues with whom he had started at Somerset House in 1805, C. W. Dilke and his brother-in-law Thomas Barrow, though he did not join them in the same office: Dickens was again in the Pay Branch, Dilke in the Navy Branch and Barrow in the Inspector's Branch. Close proximity to his brother-in-law was probably uncomfortable, bearing in mind the still outstanding debt of £213 and the circumstances under which it had been incurred.

Charles' father sought, as he had on several previous occasions, a pleasant, genteel area in which to settle with his family, and preferably a fairly new house. He found both at 16 Bayham Street, Camden Town, about three miles north of central London. The houses in the street had been erected ten years before, taking over part of the gardens of the renowned inn the Mother Red Cap, and looked down towards the city over intervening countryside. The following description of the area was written by a neighbour of the Dickens family:

Camden Town, like some other London suburbs, was but a village. Bayham-street had grass struggling through the newly-paved road. There were not more than some twenty, or, at most, thirty newly-erected houses in it. These were occupied by No. 1, Mr. Lever, the builder of the houses; No. 2, Mr. Engelheart, a then celebrated engraver; No. 3, a Captain Blake; No. 4, a retired linendraper, one of the 'old school'; No. 5, by my father and his family; No. 6, by a retired diamond merchant, two of whose sons have made their mark, one as an artist and another as the author of 'True to the core'. At No. 7 lived a retired hairdresser, who, like most others there, had a lease of his house. In another lived a Regent-street jeweller . . . Mr. Lever's field was at the back of the principal row of houses, in which haymaking was enjoyed in its season, and it was, indeed, a beautiful walk across the fields to Copenhagen House. Camden-road then was not. The village watchman's box was at one end of the street by the Red Cap tea-garden. 'Old Lorimer', who lived in Queen-street – then with gardens and a field in front of but one row of houses – was the only constable.[1]

Village it may have been, but, as Cruikshank illustrated in 1821, it could also be a rowdy area.

John Dickens' name first appears in the rate books for the half-year 5 April to 29 September 1822, for which he paid only half the sum due, indicating likely occupation from 25 June.[2] This is earlier than past biographers have supposed, though the evidence of the rate books has always been available and was made use of in relation to this and other addresses by Kitton.[3]

Their new house was not large, comprising a basement, two rooms at ground level, two on the first floor and a very small garret; a wash-house was situated at the rear. Into this limited space crammed the two elder Dickenses, James Lamert, the Dickens children Fanny, Letitia, Frederick and Alfred, and the unnamed orphan brought with the family from the Chatham workhouse. Charles was still in Chatham, as described in the last chapter. 16 Bayham Street was clearly crowded, but this was not unusual, either for the Dickens family or for families generally at this time. A deaf old woman was found who would wait on the family, serving delicate hashes of walnut ketchup, though it seems unlikely that she lived in.

Since there is no documentary evidence it is very difficult to ascertain the date that Charles was brought from Chatham to London, but as explained in the last chapter the most likely time seems to have been just after the death of his aunt, Mary Lamert, which occurred in September 1822; this is some three to six months earlier than generally supposed. This was also the end of the Michaelmas quarter of the year, when school fees, like most other regular commitments, became due for payment. Even if the Michaelmas fee was paid by John Dickens – and having left

Chatham it must have been most tempting not to pay it – it is unlikely that he would have committed himself to a further quarter, or that his wife would want to stay separated from Charles for another three months.

Whether or not John Dickens paid the school fees, it is certain that there were other outstanding financial commitments at Chatham that were left unsettled: certainly the £213 owing to Thomas Barrow, but others besides, that hung like a cloud over the family. When Charles arrived home the atmosphere was not good. Dickens' own words, supplied by Forster, give the most vivid account of life in the household at this time. Speaking of his father, Dickens said:

> in the ease of his temper, and the straitness of his means, he appeared to have utterly lost at this time the idea of educating me at all, and to have utterly put from him the notion that I had any claim upon him, in that regard, whatever. So I degenerated into cleaning his boots of a morning, and my own; and making myself useful in the work of the little house; and looking after my younger brothers and sisters (we were now six in all); and going on such poor errands as arose out of our poor way of living.[4]

The young boy obviously took the wrench from Chatham very much to heart, probably missing more than anything the companionship of his schoolfriends there and the attention that he had been receiving from his schoolmaster. If that trait in his character which, later in life, demanded the attention of those around him was at this time developing within him, then the deflation of those early days in Bayham Street must have come as a severe blow to his pride. He found it difficult to mix with the other boys in the area, possibly because as a newcomer, and as one whose father was conspicuously in financial difficulty, he had little status in their company. Among children of parents with respectable backgrounds he may have seemed, or felt, a little beneath them, particularly since he did not attend school. This hurt very much: 'As I thought . . . in the little back-garret in Bayham-street, of all I had lost in Chatham, what would I have given, if I had anything to give, to have been sent back to any other school, to have been taught something, anywhere!'[5]

It seems likely that John Dickens' sense of possible high

achievement for himself, usually brought to grief by poor financial management, was encouraged in his children: witness the seed planted in Charles' mind concerning Gads Hill Place. For a young lad nursing personal ambition, deprivation at home and the withdrawal of schooling – together with the praise and encouragement that had previously gone with it – came as twin bitter blows.

Nevertheless, there were brighter moments too. James Lamert built a toy theatre for the boy, which no doubt gave opportunity for his imagination to create worlds and scenes far from the reality of Camden Town. Then, gradually, he began to learn the attractions of living close to the heart of the metropolis. Occasionally there were visits to his Grandmother Dickens, whom we have earlier seen him describe as a grim and unsympathetic old personage, flavoured with musty dry lavender and dressed in black crape. She lived in Oxford Street, and on one such visit to her he was invested with a silver watch.[6] His grandmother may have taken the opportunities provided by these visits to tell him a little about his grandfather William, though it is difficult to find any confirmation of this. One author quotes just once from Dickens on grandfathers, in chapter one of *Martin Chuzzlewit*: 'this question was put to him, in a distinct, solemn, and formal way: "Toby Chuzzlewit, who was your grandfather?" To which he, with his last breath, no less distinctly, solemnly, and formally replied: . . . "The Lord No Zoo".' Thus with young Charles.

He probably enjoyed more than this the visits to his godfather, Christopher Huffam, who was a rigger and a mast, oar and block-maker, living in some comfort at Church Row, Limehouse, about four and a half miles from central London on the Thames. Christopher Huffam was kind to the child who carried his surname, and on visits there the young lad would be asked to perform the comic singing that he had learned in Chatham, urged on no doubt by his proud father and encouraged by the accolades of at least one guest at the house, who declared him to be a prodigy. The journeys to and from Limehouse, through the fascinating streets of London, were a joy and marvel to the boy.

The city fascinated him, providing perhaps, in contrast to Camden Town, a suitable substitute for the bustle of Chatham. In particular he was drawn to the areas of Covent Garden and the Strand.

Covent Garden market, and the avenues leading to it, are thronged with carts of all sorts, sizes, and descriptions, from the heavy lumbering waggon, with its four stout horses, to the jingling costermonger's cart with its consumptive donkey. The pavement is already strewed with decayed cabbage-leaves, broken haybands, and all the indescribable litter of a vegetable market; men are shouting, carts backing, horses neighing, boys fighting, basket-women talking, piemen expatiating on the excellence of their pastry, and donkeys braying. These and a hundred other sounds form a compound discordant enough to a Londoner's ears, and remarkably disagreeable to those of country gentlemen who are sleeping at the Hummums for the first time.[7]

He was even more attracted to the repulsive area of Seven Dials.

. . . streets of dirty, straggling houses, with now and then an unexpected court composed of buildings as ill-proportioned and deformed as the half-naked children that wallow in the kennels. Here and there, a little dark chandler's shop, with a cracked bell hung up behind the door to announce the entrance of a customer, or betray the presence of some young gentleman in whom a passion for shop tills has developed itself at an early age: others, as if for support, against some handsome lofty building, which usurps the place of a low dingy public-house; long rows of broken and patched windows expose plants that may have flourished when 'The Dials' were built, in vessels as dirty as 'The Dials' themselves; and shops for the purchase of rags, bones, old iron, and kitchen-stuff, vie in cleanliness with the bird-fanciers and rabbit-dealers, which one might fancy so many arks, but for the irresistable conviction that no bird in its proper senses, who was permitted to leave one of them, would ever come back again. Brokers' shops, which would seem to have been established by humane individuals, as refuges for destitute bugs, interspersed with announcements of day-schools, penny theatres, petition-writers, mangles, and music for balls or routs, complete the 'still-life' of the subject; and dirty men, filthy women, squalid children, fluttering shuttlecocks, noisy battledores, reeking pipes, bad fruit, more than doubtful oysters, attenuated cats, depressed dogs, and anatomical fowls, are its cheerful accompaniments.[8]

He later remarked to John Forster: 'What wild visions of prodigies of wickedness, want, and beggary, arose in my mind out of that place!'[9]

One particular visit to the city made a vivid impression on him and later became the subject of an article called 'Gone astray':

It was in the spring-time [1823] when these tender notions of mine, bursting forth into new shoots under the influence of the season, became sufficiently troublesome to my parents and guardians to occasion Somebody to volunteer to take me to see the outside of Saint Giles's Church, which was considered likely (I suppose) to quench my romantic fire, and bring me to a practical state. We set off after breakfast. I have an impression that Somebody was got up in a striking manner – in cord breeches of fine texture and milky hue, in long jean gaiters, in a green coat with bright buttons, in a blue neckerchief, and a monstrous shirt-collar. I think he must have newly come (as I had myself) out of the hop-grounds of Kent. I considered him the glass of fashion and the mould of form: a very Hamlet without the burden of his difficult family affairs.

We were conversational together, and saw the outside of Saint Giles's Church with sentiments of satisfaction, much enhanced by a flag flying from the steeple. I infer that we then went down to Northumberland House in the Strand to view the celebrated lion over the gateway. At all events, I know that in the act of looking up with mingled awe and admiration at that famous animal I lost Somebody.

The child's unreasoning terror of being lost, comes as freshly on me now as it did then. I verily believe that if I had found myself astray at the North Pole instead of in the narrow, crowded, inconvenient street over which the lion in those days presided, I could not have been more horrified. But, this first fright expended itself in a little crying and tearing up and down; and then I walked, with a feeling of dismal dignity upon me, into a court, and sat down on a step to consider how to get through life.

To the best of my belief, the idea of asking my way home never came into my head. It is possible that I may, for the time, have preferred the dismal dignity of being lost; but I have a serious conviction that in the wide scope of my arrangements for the future, I had no eyes for the nearest and most obvious course.

. . . I made up my little mind to seek my fortune. When I had found it, I thought I would drive home in a coach and six, and claim my bride. I cried a little more at the idea of such a triumph, but soon dried my eyes and came out of the court to pursue my plans.

He then describes his day of wandering the streets, managing, with what remained of a half-crown birthday present from Christopher Huffam, to feed himself and visit the theatre. However, with the arrival of darkness and rain he becomes tearful again and runs about looking for, and eventually finding, a watchman to help him.

We got at last to the watch-house, a warm and drowsy sort of place embellished with great-coats and rattles hanging up. When a paralytic messenger had been sent to make inquiries about me, I fell asleep by the fire, and awoke no more until my eyes opened on my father's face. This is literally and exactly how I went astray. They used to say I was an odd child, and I suppose I was.[10]

Other visits were made to see his uncle, Thomas Barrow, who had taken for his lodgings the upper part of a house owned by a bookseller in Gerrard Street, Soho. In 1814 he had had the bad luck to break his leg while alighting from a Hackney coach in the courtyard of Somerset House,[11] and although the break was set, another fall resulted in a compound fracture in the same place, which incapacitated him for several years and eventually resulted in a necessary amputation of the leg.[12] It was during this period of incapacity that Charles was taken to visit him. The bookseller in whose house Barrow lodged, a gentleman by the name of Manson, died in 1812, but Manson's widow carried on the business and was attracted to young Charles, lending him such books as Jane Porter's *Scottish Chiefs*, Holbein's *Dance of Death* and George Colman's *Broad Grins*. The boy was taken with these books, especially by a description of Covent Garden in one of them. He was fascinated, too, by a barber who came from nearby Dean Street to shave his uncle and who constantly reviewed the Napoleonic Wars, pointing out Napoleon's mistakes. It has been suggested that this barber was the father of the artist Turner, and such was the attraction that Charles wrote a description of him and accompanied it with a description of the old lady who waited on them at Bayham Street. Though he thought his writing extremely clever, he never had the courage to show it to anyone.[13]

It was probably on such visits to Gerrard Street that Fanny was taken along to the eminent pianoforte maker Thomas Tomkisson, who had a shop in the same road as the barber, Dean Street; for it was Tomkisson who recommended and nominated Fanny to become a pupil at the Royal Academy of Music at Hanover Square in London. Coincidentally it was in Hanover Square that her paternal grandparents had been married 42 years before. She was admitted as a boarder at the Academy on 9 April 1823, and Charles later confessed that it was a stab to his heart, thinking of his own disregarded condition, to see her go away to begin her education amid the tearful good wishes of everybody in the house. This was indeed a bitter disappointment, but probably turned the child to seek even more than before stimulation from his own resources. The independence and inner strength of his adult character can be seen to have grown out of the adversity of such childhood situations.

He was concerned, too, that his parents were talking in crisis terms of their financial difficulties. Debts were building up with local tradesmen and rates became overdue: the poor rate for the half-year ending 4 April 1823 was paid only after a summons was issued. The next half-year, up to 29 September 1823, was even more difficult, with another summons being issued for the poor rate and the watching, lighting and paving rate going ignored.[14]

Although John Dickens was enjoying a good salary at £350 a year, this was a drop from his income of £440 at Chatham, and it is difficult to know what commitments he had. Those that are known about were not heavy: the rent at Bayham Street was just £22 a year and the rates less than £4; tuition and board fees for Fanny at the Royal Academy of Music were 38 guineas a year.[15] Nevertheless, somehow the amount he earned did not equal the amount he spent, and it was decided in September 1823[16] that an additional source of income should be sought. The idea was, it seems, that Mrs Dickens should set up a school in a grand newly-built house in Gower Street North – closer to the centre of London – and that pupils would be enrolled from, among others, the East Indian connections of Christopher Huffam. It was a scheme, they believed, that was to make them rich. They moved into the splendid new neighbourhood – generally the resort of gentry and professional men – at Christmas 1823 and announced their arrival with a large brass plate on the door which read MRS DICKENS'S ESTABLISHMENT.

The Bayham Street home they left behind was renumbered 141 in 1866 and demolished in 1910. The road now carries much heavy traffic and the site of the house, marked by a plaque erected by the Dickens Fellowship, is covered by a building of the Camden and Islington Area Health Authority. A garret window from the building was saved from demolition and is held by the Dickens House Museum at Doughty Street in London.

4 GOWER STREET NORTH

The house at Gower Street North was described as comfortable, with six rooms, those facing the front having two windows to each room; the kitchen was in the basement and there was no garden.[17] The new start in life was made with a wave of optimism and activity: 'I left at a great many other doors, a great many circulars calling attention to the merits of the establishment', Charles wrote. But the wave of optimism soaked into a beach of uninterest: 'nobody ever came to school, nor do I recollect that anybody ever proposed to come, or that the least preparation was made to receive anybody'.[18] The Dickenses rapidly lost control of the situation, not only incurring new expenses at Gower Street but, bearing in mind a debt of £40 due to a baker at Camden Town that later came to light, apparently bringing with them all their old debts.

Dickens' own description of this deteriorating period of his life compares extremely closely with part of the history of David Copperfield – the fact being put to paper by Dickens two or three years before the fiction.[19] In the latter Copperfield describes vividly the atmosphere at home:

The only visitors I ever saw, or heard of, were creditors. *They* used to come at all hours, and some of them were quite ferocious. One dirty-faced man, I think he was a bootmaker, used to edge himself into the passage as early as seven o'clock in the morning, and call up the stairs to Mr. Micawber – 'Come! You ain't out yet, you know. Pay us, will you? You just pay us, d'ye hear? Come!' Receiving no answer to these taunts, he would mount in his wrath to the words 'swindlers' and 'robbers'; and these being ineffectual too, would sometimes go to the extremity of crossing the street, and roaring up at the windows of the second floor, where he knew Mr. Micawber was. At these times, Mr. Micawber would be transported with grief and mortification, even to the length (as I was once made aware by a scream from his wife) of making motions at himself with a razor; but within half-an-hour afterwards, he would polish up his shoes with extraordinary pains, and go out, humming a tune with a greater air of gentility than ever. Mrs. Micawber was quite as elastic. I have known her to be thrown into fainting fits by the King's taxes at three o'clock, and to eat lamb chops, breaded, and drink warm ale (paid for with two tea-spoons that had gone to the pawnbroker's) at four. On one occasion, when an execution had just been put in, coming home through some chance as early as six o'clock, I saw her lying . . . under the grate in a swoon, with her hair all torn about her face; but I never knew her more cheerful than she was, that very same night, over a veal cutlet before the kitchen fire, telling me stories about her papa and mama, and the company they used to keep.[20]

Having failed to gain an income from Mrs Dickens's Establishment, the family looked around for other means to earn money, and they were pleased when an offer of employment for Charles was made, bringing with it an income of six or seven shillings a week. It came from James Lamert, who had lived with them at Chatham and Bayham Street, and was now managing the shoe-blacking business of Warren's at 30 Hungerford Stairs. It was an offer made out of kindness: Lamert and Charles (always bearing in mind their age difference) had in the past got on well together, and there was pity on Lamert's part for Charles' situation at home and for the family's deteriorating circumstances. Indeed it was not unusual at that time for children of Charles' age to be sent out to work – taking the country as a whole, regular work generally began at the age of seven or eight.[21] But for Charles, who had been cherishing hopes of growing up to be a learned and distinguished man, the unexpected move was a nasty shock.

The question of the date of his commencement at Warren's has received some attention. Forster supplies no date, yet implies that it was after the move to Gower Street (26 December 1823) and before John Dickens' arrest (20 February 1824): that is, both

Forster and Dickens write at this stage of their narratives of the Bayham Street home in the past tense; and Dickens writes of his parents taking together the decision for him to go to Warren's. It can be judged that the family would have allowed some weeks to have passed after their removal to Gower Street North before accepting that the proposed school was going to be a complete failure and that Charles would have to go to work. This narrows the likely date to a period between the end of January and 20 February. Kitton and Langton can suggest no date, yet Storey[22] tells us that it was a fortnight before John Dickens was arrested, and Edgar Johnson,[23] knowing that he started on a Monday, has arrived at 9 February, two days after his twelfth birthday. The flaw in this argument is that Storey based her book on conversations with Dickens' daughter Kate, and yet it is widely reported and accepted that his children knew nothing at all of the warehouse period until they read it in Forster's book. Therefore Kate could not have had the information from her father; the only other possible sources for Kate's information would have been either Forster, who had he known it would almost certainly have used such a poignant date in his book, or her mother, who had heard the autobiographical fragment from Dickens' own lips.[24] The date of 9 February does, under all the circumstances, seem to be the most likely date.

With some sensitivity Lamert situated Charles in the counting house on the first floor of the factory, away from the working-class boys downstairs, even though he did the same work as they; and he organised to teach Charles every day during the dinner hour. But all this just softened the blow; and the good intentions, with time, gradually faded. Dickens' own account of this period is both informative and moving:

> The blacking warehouse was the last house on the left-hand side of the way, at old Hungerford-stairs. It was a crazy, tumble-down old house, abutting of course on the river, and literally overrun with rats. Its wainscotted rooms, and its rotten floors and staircase, and the old grey rats swarming down in the cellars, and the sound of their squeaking and scuffling coming up the stairs at all times, and the dirt and decay of the place, rise up visibly before me, as if I were there again. The counting-house was on the first floor, looking over the coal-barges and the river. There was a recess in it, in which I was to

sit and work. My work was to cover the pots of paste-blacking; first with a piece of oil-paper, and then with a piece of blue paper; to tie them round with a string; and then to clip the paper close and neat, all round, until it looked as smart as a pot of ointment from an apothecary's shop. When a certain number of grosses of pots had attained this pitch of perfection, I was to paste on each a printed label; and then go on again with more pots. Two or three other boys were kept at similar duty down stairs on similar wages. One of them came up, in a ragged apron and a paper cap, on the first Monday morning, to show me the trick of using the string and tying the knot. His name was Bob Fagin; and I took the liberty of using his name, long afterwards, in *Oliver Twist*.

Our relative had kindly arranged to teach me something in the dinner-hour; from twelve to one, I think it was; every day. But an arrangement so incompatible with counting-house business soon died away, from no fault of his or mine; and for the same reason, my small work-table, and my grosses of pots, my papers, string, scizzors, paste-pot, and labels, by little and little, vanished out of the recess in the counting-house, and kept company with the other small work-tables, grosses of pots, papers, string, scizzors, and paste-pots, down stairs. It was not long, before Bob Fagin and I, and another boy whose name was Paul Green, but who was currently believed to have been christened Poll (a belief which I transferred, long afterwards again, to Mr. Sweedlepipe, in *Martin Chuzzlewit*), worked generally, side by side. Bob Fagin was an orphan, and lived with his brother-in-law, a waterman. Poll Green's father had the additional distinction of being a fireman, and was employed at Drury-lane theatre; where another relation of Poll's, I think his little sister, did imps in the pantomimes.

No words can express the secret agony of my soul as I sunk into this companionship; compared these every day associates with those of my happier childhood; and felt my early hopes of growing up to be a learned and distinguished man, crushed in my breast. The deep remembrance of the sense I had of being utterly neglected and hopeless; of the shame I felt in my position; of the misery it was to my young heart to believe that, day by day, what I had learned, and thought, and delighted in, and raised my fancy and my emulation up by, was passing away from me, never to be brought back any more; cannot be written. My whole nature was so penetrated with the grief and humiliation of such considerations, that even now, famous and caressed and happy, I often forget in my dreams that I have a dear wife and children; even that I am a man; and wander desolately back to that time of my life.[25]

The situation at home was as depressing as that at work, and eventually devastating, as Forster reports:

'I know that we got on very badly with the butcher and baker; that very often we had not too much for dinner; and that at last my father was arrested.'[26] The interval between the sponging-house and the prison was passed by the sorrowful lad in running errands and carrying messages for the prisoner, delivered with swollen eyes and through shining tears; and the last words said to him by his father before he was finally carried to the Marshalsea, were to the effect that the sun was set upon him for ever. 'I really believed at the time,' said Dickens to me, 'that they had broken my heart.'[27]

The heartbreak deepened as Charles went to see his father in prison:

My father was waiting for me in the lodge, and we went up to his room (on the top story but one), and cried very much. And he told me, I remember, to take warning by the Marshalsea, and to observe that if a man had twenty pounds a-year, and spent nineteen pounds nineteen shillings and sixpence, he would be happy; but that a shilling spent the other way would make him wretched.[28]

Charles helped to sell off smaller items from the Gower Street home to provide money; and eventually the larger items went too, as described in *David Copperfield*:

I don't know how the household furniture came to be sold for the family benefit, or who sold it, except that I did not. Sold it was, however, and carried away in a van; except the bed, a few chairs, and the kitchen table. With these possessions we encamped, as it were, in two parlours of the emptied house in Windsor Terrace; Mrs. Micawber, the children, the Orfling, and

myself; and lived in those rooms night and day. I have no idea
for how long, though it seems to me for a long time. At last
Mrs. Micawber resolved to move into the prison, where Mr.
Micawber had now secured a room to himself. So I took the key
of the house to the landlord, who was very glad to get it.[29]

It is very difficult to fix the date that Mrs Dickens gave up the
Gower Street North home. It must have been some time after 2
March, when John Dickens used the address in a letter to the
Admiralty, and before 28 May, when he was released from the
Marshalsea (Mrs Dickens, like Mrs Micawber, took her family to
live in the prison for a while). A note is made in the rate book that
Mrs Dickens would be staying until Midsummer – 24 June – but
this was clearly not adhered to. A considered date of removal is 4
April, when the quarterly rent of £12 10s became due.

The Dickens family were the very first occupants of 4 Gower
Street North, but their stay was clearly a short one. In 1864 the
address changed to 147 Gower Street; it was then purchased and
demolished by Maples Store in the 1890s. The site is now covered
partly by the University College Hospital and partly by an office
block. There is no known illustration or photograph of this
building.

37 LITTLE COLLEGE STREET, CAMDEN TOWN

While Mrs Dickens, together with Letitia, aged 8, Frederick, 3,
and Alfred, 2, moved into the prison and the little servant girl
from the Chatham workhouse was put into lodgings nearby,
Charles was granted some kind of special treatment, by being
placed with an old friend of the family, Mrs Roylance of Little
College Street, Camden Town – close to his old home in Bayham
Street. Charles always believed he was a lodger, guessing that his
father paid for the room; but the old lady's granddaughter later
pointed out that the Dickens family were always friends and
welcome, invited guests.[30]

Dickens left a vivid description of his day-to-day existence at
this time:

She had a little brother and sister under her care then;
somebody's natural children, who were very irregularly paid

for; and a widow's little son. The two boys and I slept in the same room. My own exclusive breakfast, of a penny cottage loaf and a pennyworth of milk, I provided for myself. I kept another small loaf, and a quarter of a pound of cheese, on a particular shelf of a particular cupboard; to make my supper on when I came back at night. They made a hole in the six or seven shillings, I know well; and I was out at the blacking-warehouse all day, and had to support myself upon that money all the week. I suppose my lodging was paid for, by my father. I certainly did not pay it myself; and I certainly had no other assistance whatever (the making of my clothes, I think, excepted), from Monday morning until Saturday night. No advice, no counsel, no encouragement, no consolation, no support, from any one that I can call to mind, so help me God.

Sundays, Fanny and I passed in the prison. I was at the academy in Tenterden-street, Hanover-square, at nine o'clock in the morning, to fetch her; and we walked back there together, at night.

I was so young and childish, and so little qualified – how could I be otherwise? – to undertake the whole charge of my own existence, that, in going to Hungerford-stairs of a morning, I could not resist the stale pastry put out at half-price on trays at the confectioners' doors in Tottenham-court-road; and I often spent in that, the money I should have kept for my dinner. Then I went without my dinner, or bought a roll, or a slice of pudding. There were two pudding shops between which I was divided, according to my finances. One was in a court close to St. Martin's-church (at the back of the church) which is now removed altogether. The pudding at that shop was made with currants, and was rather a special pudding, but was dear: two penn'orth not being larger than a penn'orth of more ordinary pudding. A good shop for the latter was in the Strand, somewhere near where the Lowther-arcade is now. It was a stout, hale pudding, heavy and flabby; with great raisins in it, stuck in whole, at great distances apart. It came up hot, at about noon every day; and many and many a day did I dine off it.

We had half-an-hour, I think, for tea. When I had money enough, I used to go to a coffee-shop, and have half-a-pint of coffee, and a slice of bread and butter. When I had no money, I took a turn in Covent-garden market, and stared at the pineapples. The coffee-shops to which I most resorted were, one in Maiden-lane; one in a court (non-existant now) close to Hungerford-market; and one in St. Martin's-lane, of which I only recollect that it stood near the church, and that in the door there was an oval glass-plate, with COFFEE-ROOM painted on it, addressed towards the street. If I ever find myself in a very different kind of coffee-room now, but where there is such an inscription on glass, and read it backward on the wrong side MOOR-EEFFOC (as I often used to do then, in a dismal reverie), a shock goes through my blood.

I know I do not exaggerate, unconsciously and unintentionally, the scantiness of my resources and the difficulties of my life. I know that if a shilling or so were given me by any one, I spent it in a dinner or a tea. I know that I worked, from morning to night, with common men and boys, a shabby child. I know that I tried, but ineffectually, not to anticipate my money, and to make it last the week through; by putting it away in a drawer I had in the counting-house, wrapped into six little parcels, each parcel containing the same amount, and labelled with a different day. I know that I have lounged about the streets, insufficiently and unsatisfactorily fed. I know that, but for the mercy of God, I might easily have been, for any care that was taken of me, a little robber or a little vagabond.[31]

It was thus that Charles was pushed by his parents – whether intentionally or otherwise we shall never know – into an independence that, though he resented it, was to prove such an important part of his character, and into a situation that expanded his knowledge of the London streets: his journey backwards and forwards to work was, after all, more than five miles each day, and on Sundays, when he walked his sister to and from the Music Academy and visited his mother and father in prison, he walked about twelve miles. But, no matter how much he may have been subconsciously learning about the great capital city, he did not like the journey out to an area that he subsequently described as a desolate place, surrounded by little else than fields and ditches.[32] Nor did he like being separated from his family, or the miserable blank that he was faced with at Mrs Roylance's. The blacking factory, too, was a continual strain on his sensitivity, and he continued to build an enormous resentment: against his parents, against his situation, against his prospects. He built, too, a determination to suffer in silence, and a determination to overcome the situation and achieve success. And such was the strength of his building that he shared his resentment, his silence and his determination with only two people till the day he died: his wife and his biographer.

> I never said, to man or boy, how it was that I came to be there [at Warren's], or gave the least indication of being sorry that I was there. That I suffered in secret, and that I suffered exquisitely, no one ever knew but I. How much I suffered, it is, as I have said already, utterly beyond my power to tell. No man's imagination can overstep the reality. But I kept my own counsel, and I did my work.[33]

How long Charles tolerated his room at Little College Street it is impossible to say with complete accuracy, but his description of this time, and his period at the following address, imply a number of weeks in each case. Since departure from Gower Street North has been estimated at 4 April, and since it is known that John Dickens was released from the Marshalsea on 28 May, then the two addresses probably shared just eight weeks between them, or about four weeks each.

1 LANT STREET, BOROUGH

In the end the miserable existence away from his family, and in the home of a stranger, became too painful for him:

> One Sunday night I remonstrated with my father on this head, so pathetically and with so many tears, that his kind nature gave way. He began to think that it was not quite right. I do believe he had never thought so before, or thought about it. It was the first remonstrance I had ever made about my lot, and perhaps it opened up a little more than I intended. A back-attic was found for me at the house of an insolvent-court agent, who lived in Lant-street in the borough, where Bob Sawyer lodged many years afterwards. A bed and bedding were sent over for me, and made up on the floor. The little window had a pleasant prospect of a timber-yard; and when I took possession of my new abode, I thought it was paradise.[34]

Past writers on Dickens have had difficulty locating the house in Lant Street at which he lodged, but a little research has tracked it down. Early maps[35] indicate that the only timber yard in Lant Street stood behind houses on the north side of the road, and a search of street directories[36] and rate books[37] leads to the home and business address of Archibald Campbell Russell and Son, an attorney and therefore the person most likely to have been engaged as an agent for the Insolvent Court.[38] He lived in 1824 at 1 Lant Street, the number being later changed to 5,[39] and looked directly over the timber yard. Forster specifically mentions a grown-up son,[40] and Russell emphasises this in the name of his business.

An impression of Lant Street is given in *The Pickwick Papers*:

In this happy retreat are colonised a few clear-starchers, a sprinkling of journeymen bookbinders, one or two prison agents for the Insolvent Court, several small housekeepers who are employed in the Docks, a handful of mantua-makers, and a seasoning of jobbing tailors. The majority of the inhabitants either direct their energies to the letting of furnished apartments, or devote themselves to the healthful and invigorating pursuit of mangling. The chief features in the still life of the street are green shutters, lodging-bills, brass door-plates, and bell-handles; the principal specimens of animated nature, the pot-boy, the muffin youth, and the baked-potato man. The population is migratory, usually disappearing on the verge of quarter-day, and generally by night. His Majesty's revenues are seldom collected in this happy valley; the rents are dubious; and the water communication is very frequently cut off.[41]

JOHN DICKENS IN PRISON

Lant Street was probably chosen as a lodging place for Charles because it was very near to the Marshalsea Prison, where his father had been detained since 20 February. While there John Dickens continued to receive his salary from the Admiralty,[42] though this was more likely to have been on medical grounds than for any other reason. Within a fortnight of his imprisonment he had decided to apply for retirement from his position with the Navy Pay Office together with an appropriate pension, aware no doubt that should he be imprisoned for any length of time, then his employers would not continue to pay his salary, and judging that half a loaf would be better than none. In a letter headed 4 Gower Street North and dated 2 March 1824, John Dickens wrote to W. M. Huskisson, Treasurer of the Navy:

> Sir, Herewith I have the honor to enclose a Certificate of an unfortunate calamity, which renders me incapable of attending to any public duty, and have most respectfully to solicit that you will recommend me as a fit object for Superannuation.
> I have served nearly nineteen Years having been appointed by Mr. Canning in 1805, and during nearly the whole of which period Mr. Smith has been Paymaster, to whom I beg to refer you, for my general conduct and character. I am Sir Your obedient Humble Servant John Dickens.[43]

This letter was accompanied by a medical certificate:

> These are to certify that Mr. John Dickens of the Navy Pay Office is from infirmity of body, arising from a chronic infection of the Urinary Organs, incapacitated from attending to any possible duty. Signed John Pool – Surgeon 19 Dover St. Piccadilly. W. Vaughan Surgeon Kent Road.[44]

A week later Huskisson sent Dickens' letter and certificate to John Croker, the Secretary of the Admiralty, accompanied by the following letter:

> Sir, I request you to lay before the Lords Commissioners of the Admiralty the enclosed copy of a letter from Mr. John Dickens, a Clerk of the 3d Class in the Inspector's Branch of this Office, requesting Superannuation on account of being incapacitated from attending to his duty from his state of health, which letter is accompanied by the usual Medical Certificates. Mr. Dickens is now in the 19th year of his service, having been appointed in April 1805, and is in the 39th year of his age.[45]
> He has, I am informed, always discharged his duty properly, and will be entitled under the Act of 3d Geo; 4th Cap. 113 to a Pension of 5/13ths of his salary (£350) or £145:16:8.
> Mr. Dickens being entitled under the late Establishment to a higher salary for length of service (£350) than he could attain

under the present Establishment and in his present Class, a yearly saving of £114:3:4 will for some time be effected to the Public by the difference between his Pension and the Salary of a new Clerk at £90 and Mr. Dickens's Salary of £350. I am Sir Your very humble Servant W. Huskisson.[46]

How far credibility must be stretched to accept the simultaneous occurrence of John Dickens' infirmity and his imprisonment it is difficult to say; but it should be borne in mind that his death in 1851 was caused by the 'Rupture of the Urethra from old Standing Stricture and consequent Mortification of the Scrotum from infiltration of Urine'.[47] Bearing this in mind, it seems likely that John Dickens' problems in prison were indeed more than just financial.

Ironically, financial matters were a lot easier for him inside the Marshalsea than they had been outside. Here his income was large enough to provide accommodation for the family, sufficient food, the servant girl from the Chatham workhouse to wait on them throughout the day, and freedom from worrying creditors. An incident in the prison, related by Charles, and referring to a petition for the boon of a bounty to the prisoners in order to drink the health of the King on his birthday, gives a good impression of the conviviality under strained circumstances:

When I went to the Marshalsea of a night, I was always delighted to hear from my mother what she knew about the histories of the different debtors in the prison; and when I heard of this approaching ceremony, I was so anxious to see them all come in, one after another (though I knew the greater part of them already, to speak to, and they me), that I got leave of absence on purpose, and established myself in a corner, near the petition. It was stretched out, I recollect, on a great ironing-board, under the window, which in another part of the room made a bedstead at night. The internal regulations of the place, for cleanliness and order, and for the government of a common room in the ale-house; where hot water and some means of cooking, and a good fire, were provided for all who paid a very small subscription; were excellently administered by a governing committee of debtors, of which my father was chairman for the time being. As many of the principal officers of this body as could be got into the small room without filling it up, supported him, in front of the petition; and my old friend Captain Porter (who had washed himself, to do honour to so solemn an occasion) stationed himself close to it, to read it to all who were unacquainted with its contents. The door was then thrown open, and they began to come in, in a long file; several waiting on the landing outside, while one entered, affixed his signature, and went out. To everybody in succession, Captain Porter said, 'Would you like to hear it read?' If he weakly showed the least disposition to hear it, Captain Porter, in a loud sonorous voice, gave him every word of it. I remember a certain luscious roll he gave to such words as 'Majesty – gracious Majesty – your gracious Majesty's unfortunate subjects – your Majesty's well-known munificence,' – as if the words were something real in his mouth, and delicious to taste: my poor father meanwhile listening with a little of an author's vanity, and contemplating (not severely) the spikes on the opposite wall. Whatever was comical in this scene, and whatever was pathetic, I sincerely believe I perceived in my corner, whether I demonstrated or not, quite as well as I should perceive it now. I made out my own little character and story for every man who put his name to the sheet of paper. I might be able to do that now, more truly: not more earnestly, or with a closer interest. Their different peculiarities of dress, of face, of gait, of manner, were written indelibly upon my memory. I would rather have seen it than the best play ever played; and I thought about it afterwards, over the pots of paste-blacking, often and often.[48]

But life in prison could not always have been so carefree for John Dickens. Extracts given above indicate the tears – his own, and those of Charles – and no doubt there were more, shared with his wife and other children, who through his own ineptitude he had brought to prison. And he suffered that terrible infection of the urinary organs, an illness which he bore personally and in silence, as Charles later reported.[49]

RELEASE FROM PRISON

To comply with the terms for his release from prison John Dickens had to declare all his debts to the satisfaction of the Court, to hold goods valued at no more than £20 and to agree to later settle his debts if it became possible. Under the second of these terms Charles was called forward for scrutiny.

> It was necessary, as a matter of form, that the clothes I wore should be seen by the official appraiser. I had a half-holiday to enable me to call upon him, at his own time, at a house somewhere behind the Obelisk. I recollect his coming out to look at me with his mouth full, and a strong smell of beer upon him, and saying good-naturedly that 'that would do', and 'it was all right'. Certainly the hardest creditor would not have been disposed (even if he had been legally entitled) to avail himself of my poor white hat, little jacket, or corduroy trowsers. But I had a fat old silver watch in my pocket, which had been given me by my grandmother before the blacking days, and I had entertained my doubts as I went along whether that valuable possession might not bring me over the twenty pounds. So I was greatly relieved, and made him a bow of acknowledgment as I went out.[50]

During the period that arrangements for John Dickens' release were being processed the sad news came of the death of his mother; just how much she had been affected by the shame of her son's imprisonment, and whether or not the stress of the situation contributed towards her death, it will never be known. He was presumably prevented from attending the funeral.

But for John Dickens the personal tragedy was later eased when he learned that his mother had left him the sum of £450. Her will was written as follows:

> I, Elizabeth Dickens of Oxford Street in the Parish of Saint Marylebone London Widow do hereby make and declare this to be my last Will and Testament and I do hereby Nominate and Appoint my Eldest Son William Dickens to be my Executor to this my last Will and Testament.
>
> I desire that my Funeral Expences and all My Just and lawful debts be paid out of my funded property. – In the first place I give and bequeath to my said Son William Dickens the Sum of Five Hundred Pounds Stock (being part of a larger Sum of Mine now Standing in my Son William Dickens's name) in the three per Cent Consols of the Governor and Company of the Bank of England. – In the second place I give and bequeath to my

Youngest Son, John Dickens the sum of four Hundred and fifty pounds Stock (Being the remainder of my property now Standing in my son William Dickens name) in the three per Cent Consols of the Governor and Company of the Bank of England. – (The reason that I make this difference between my two Sons is, that my Son John Dickens having had from me [large]/several/Sums of Money some years ago –) – But if it should please God that I should Survive my Eldest Son William Dickens in such case I do give and bequeath my Property as follows. – First I do appoint Thos Paul Esqr of Trevor Square Knightsbridge to be one of my Executors to this my last Will and Testament and my Daughter in Law Sarah Dickens to be the Other Executrix to this my last Will and Testament and I give & bequeath in such case to my above named Executor Thomas Paul Eqr the Sum of Ten Guineas for the trouble he may be at in Executing this My last Will –

In the first place I give and bequeath to my Son John Dickens the sum of Five Hundred & fifty Pounds Stock in the three per Cent Consols of the Governor and Company of the Bank of England. – In the second place I give and bequeath to my Daughter in Law Sarah Dickens the Interest of Four Hundred pounds Stock in the three per Cent Consols of the Governor and Company of the Bank of England, for her Natural Life, and at her Decease I request that the said Four Hundred Pounds Stock in the three per Cent Consols be Sold out and Equally devided amongst my surviving Grand Children of John and Elizabeth Dickens. As to my wearing apparel I give and bequeath the same to my two Sons William Dickens and John Dickens, share and share alike.

Revoking all former Wills made by me, I do hereby declare this to be my last Will and Testament whereunto I have set my hand and Seal this Twenty fourth Day of January In the year of our Lord One Thousand Eight/Hundred/and Twenty four –
Elizth Dickens[51]

John Dickens' mother died on 26 April 1824 and she was buried on 30 April. It was to be another month before John Dickens was released from prison, on 28 May, and just a little longer before the will was proved, on 4 June. The £450 left to John Dickens was in no way responsible for his release, since he was freed before the money became available, but it did have a long-term effect.

While it is not easy to trace the details of John Dickens' financial affairs after a lapse of 160 years, it is possible at this stage to make some assessment from the few facts that are known. There is no evidence that John Dickens had financial difficulties while in Portsmouth, but it is possible that on removal to London in 1815, suffering from a drop in income, he borrowed money from his mother as indicated in her will. All evidence points, however, to tremendous problems at Chatham. In 1819 he borrowed the huge sum of £200 and promptly ran into difficulties with the repayments, so that his brother-in-law had to settle the debt. The debt, now owing to Thomas Barrow and increased to £213, was carried to London in 1822. But other debts must have been carried to London too: although John Dickens was arrested on a debt of £40 to James Karr, a baker of Camden Town, when it came to clearing his insolvency debts the repayments were made at the offices of J. Henslow in Rochester. It must be concluded, then, that there were more debts in Rochester, and possibly of greater amounts than those incurred in London.

According to the terms for release his legacy would have been paid direct to the assignee appointed by the court, in order to pay off his debts. Since the first of these repayments, made on 2 November 1825, did not conclude the proceedings, it must be assumed that £450 was not sufficient and that John Dickens had debts in excess of that amount. The second payment, made on 13 November 1826, did clear the amounts owing, but from the little that is known of John Dickens between November 1825 and November 1826 it would seem that he would have had little opportunity to save much money, and it can be surmised that the second payment did not involve a large sum. The total amount of debt, then, was probably £500 or a little more. In addition, consideration must be given to Thomas Barrow's loan of £213. Since this sum was never repaid it must be assumed that it was not declared to the Insolvency Court, agreement having been obtained from Barrow to keep the matter within the family. Such a family agreement is referred to in *David Copperfield*:

> Mr. Micawber's affairs, although past their crisis, were very much involved by reasons of a certain 'Deed', of which I used to hear a great deal . . . At last this document appeared to be got out of the way, somehow; at all events it ceased to be the rock a-head it had been; and Mrs. Micawber informed me that

'her family' had decided that Mr. Micawber should apply for his release under the Insolvent Debtors' Act, which would set him free, she expected, in about six weeks.[52]

This amount brings the total debt to more than £700. This was a very large sum and it is fascinating to ponder on how it was spent, bearing in mind that it would be the equivalent of about £21 500 at 1987 prices.

At the beginning of this book I pointed out that William Dickens could not have conceived the profound effect on the world that his own life would ultimately have. The same was true of his wife, even though she survived him by 39 years. Lying on her deathbed she would almost certainly have considered her first son, William, to have been the true success of the family, owning as he did his own small business, and with a good sum of money invested with the Bank of England. Sad to say, for her, he had no children. On the other hand little good could have come, she might have thought, from her second son, who, with his large family, had always caused problems and now, shame of shames, had landed himself and her grandchildren in prison. She could never have imagined the fame that would be bestowed on the Dickens name through her idle and incapable son John, and it is sad to think that she passed unknowing from this world to the next.

Charles must have looked forward to moving out of Lant Street; and yet he seemed to retain some affection for the place, probably returning there as an adult, when he was writing *The Pickwick Papers*, to look again at the humble lodgings that he once thought were Paradise. They were still standing then and stood for over 150 years more, being demolished as recently as 1974. The layout of the immediate area is still remarkably similar to that of 1824, while the district celebrates its brief involvement with the author by using such names as the Charles Dickens Primary School, Dickens Square, Weller Street, Pickwick Street, Quilp Street, Copperfield Street and Sawyer Street. But the euphoria of being out of Lant Street and back with his family was, for the young Charles, tinged with bitterness, since there was no sign at this stage of his being taken away from Warren's.

5

Release from Prison, Release from Warren's and Back to School

LITTLE COLLEGE STREET AGAIN

On release from the Marshalsea Prison on 28 May 1824 John Dickens turned once again to that friend of the family, Mrs Roylance, for accommodation,[1] though for how long the Dickens family took advantage of this friendship it is impossible to say: there is no rent book, they were not rate-payers, so do not appear in the rate books, and no biographers or acquaintances have left the slightest hint. It seems likely that soon after John Dickens' release the family parted company with the servant girl from the Chatham workhouse: after the Marshalsea she is not mentioned again by Forster, and in *David Copperfield* the Orfling – whom she very closely resembled – said goodbye to David and the Micawbers just one week after Micawber's release from prison, her fate, David presumed, being a return to the workhouse.[2] Whether the girl did in fact get back to Chatham, or had to make her own way as a lone child in the harsh wickedness of London, we shall never know. It seems a hard fate if this latter situation were so, and especially since she probably never even had the small comfort of knowing that she left her mark on Dickens, and certainly never knew that he left at least some resemblance of her that would last and be enjoyed by many people over many years.

Most house removals at this period were carried out on the year's Quarter Days, rents and rates being set and paid by the quarter, and this is the best guidance available for setting a limit on the Dickens family's stay with Mrs Roylance. The stay was likely to be either for one month, until 24 June, or for four months, until 29 September. Either date is possible, though the earlier one seems more likely, if only because the whole Dickens

96

family would have proved quite a handful for the good-natured Mrs Roylance.

The name of Little College Street was changed in 1828 to College Street West and the portion north of King Street was changed again in 1887, this time to College Place, by which it is now known. Number 37 was renumbered 130 and was demolished in 1890, when the street was rebuilt. There is no known photograph or illustration of 37 Little College Street.

HAMPSTEAD

Forster reports that the family moved on from Mrs Roylance's to a house in Hampstead, a little further north of London.[3] No other authority on Dickens has supplied evidence of this home, though some have repeated Forster. Neither have I been able to provide additional information: a search of the rate books covering Hampstead was made for the quarter March 1824, but nothing was found, and the next available rate book is for Sepember 1825, which is much too late. It is possible that they stayed with a Mrs Davis at North End, Hampstead, since this is a confirmed address for John Dickens in 1834 and a probable address for Charles in 1832.

It could not have been an easy time for the twelve-year-old boy and his father, since they must have travelled between Hampstead and the Strand each day, a lengthy round journey of ten miles. If John Dickens was still suffering somewhat from his 'chronic infection of the Urinary Organs' then this must have been an uncomfortable daily journey for him. And since Charles was travelling to his unpleasant task at Warren's it would have held little pleasure for the youngster either. Such a journey was not uncommon, though: John Dickens and his son Alfred were in the same position some years later, in 1834,[4] and Charles was walking the journey himself in 1832.[5]

However, the situation was not to continue long, since John Dickens was busy pressing his claim for retirement from the Navy Pay Office. On 8 December 1824 William Huskisson wrote to John Croker, the Secretary of the Admiralty:

Sir   In reference to my letter to you of the 9th March last, & of Mr. Barrow's answer of the 11th respecting the Superannuation of Mr. Dickens of this Office, I beg leave to state that there are circumstances in his case which, I trust, will warrant me in requesting, & their Lordships acceding to that measure – They are of a mixed nature, arising partly from the nature, of his complaint, which altho' it does not altogether incapacitate, frequently interrupts him in the discharge of his duty; and partly from his private Embarrassments – After an imprisonment of 3 months, he has been compelled to take the benefit of the Insolvent Debtors Act, and he had previously transmitted to me Medical Certificates of his inability, & applied for retirement. – Under this combination of untoward circumstances, I am equally unwilling that he should remain in Office, or be entirely dismissed without provision, for he can plead a service of near 20 Years, and a Wife & family of 6 children totally dependent on his income for life – Looking therefore to Mr. Dickens's services, and to the utter destitution to which his family must be thrown by his dismissal without some provision, I put it to their Lordship's compassionate consideration, whether it be not a case which may be submitted to the Treasury on it's special circumstances, under the 5th part of the Act of the 3rd of Geo. 4th ch. 113, that an allowance may be granted in proportion to his length of service.

There will be no danger of a precedent to persons under similar circumstances, as I shall immediately make a regulation in the Office, that hereafter Clerks attempting to take benefit of the Insolvent Act shall be discharged from their situation, which regulation I consider to be necessary, not only for the General respectability of a Public Office, but particularly called for in mine which involves so much pecuniary responsibility.

As Mr. Dickins would have completed the 20 Year of his Service on 5th of April next, his rate of Superannuation according to his present salary, (£350) would amount to £145.16.8 which I anxiously hope may be granted to Him under the special circumstances which I have now stated.[6]

29 JOHNSON STREET, SOMERS TOWN

John Dickens began to plan a new future for himself and his family, starting with a home in Johnson Street, Somers Town.[7] Somers Town was a new but not particularly attractive residential area. Up to the last decade of the eighteenth century it had been almost exclusively rural, providing uninterrupted views from south of the Euston Road across to Hampstead; but then building across this large open area was carried out between 1790 and 1840, Johnson Street itself being created about 1796.[8] Hone's Year Book of 1832 reported: 'Somers Town, isolated and sunny as it was when I first haunted it, is now little better than another arm to the great Briareus, dingy with smoke and deprived, almost wholly, of the gardens and fields which once seemed to me to render it a terrestrial paradise.'[9] The Dickenses when they moved in were more fortunate than some, since their house overlooked extensive fields at the rear, providing a suitable play area for the children and their friends.

The house itself was not particularly attractive: faced with brick (to which plaster was later added), it was separated from the pavement only by a small square of concrete and an iron railing. The small doorway, topped by an arched fanlight, guarded a narrow passage that ran the depth of the house down to the back door, the passage being divided half way down by a small arch with fluted architraves. Situated off the passage were the front parlour, the back kitchen and a wooden stairway, leading to the first-floor landing. On the first floor were two rooms which had the advantage of possible conversion to one large apartment by opening dividing double doors. From the back window there was a good view across the fields to Camden Town. After doubling back from the first floor flight of stairs, a second flight led from the first-floor landing to a second floor, which was divided into a large front room and a small back room. Above was a roomy attic. It seems very likely that the original wall decorations were huge marble squares, which appeared everywhere from the front door to the top of the house.[10] The small back yard was half taken up with a lean-to and a wash-house, the latter having a copper built in; and the high garden walls between the rest of the yards in the street were broken to allow a flow of air. Behind the back wall stretched fields belonging to the Duke of Bedford's estate, and embedded in the wall was a boundary stone with the inscription 'D. of B.'.[11]

Biographers estimating the date of removal to Johnson Street have leaned heavily on Kitton's inaccurate reading of the rate books and have given the date as summer 1824.[12] However, the evidence from the rate books must be examined very closely,[13] and even then firm conclusions cannot be drawn. The rate for the half year to Michaelmas 1824 (29 September) was made on 14 July and would have been collected between that date and Michaelmas Day. This rate book shows that 29 Johnson Street[14] was empty and tells us that the tenant who had left the premises was Caroline Weldon. No new tenant is given. The rate for the next half year, ending Lady Day 1825 (25 March) was made on 19 January 1825 and collected between that date and Lady Day. The rate book lists at 29 Johnson Street Caroline Dickens, but has Dickens crossed through, Weldon entered, then Weldon crossed through and Dickens re-entered (see Plate 17). There would seem, then, to have been some confusion over the occupancy, or over the period of occupancy within the half year – and therefore the responsibility for paying the rate. Since rents were paid quarterly, and most house moving was carried out around Quarter Days, it seems likely that the Dickens family moved into Johnson Street at the beginning of the Lady Quarter, the last week of December 1824. Hence the confusion over responsibility for the rate for the whole half year. There has been confusion, too, concerning the entry in the rate books of the name of Caroline Dickens. This is clearly a clerical error, the first name of Caroline Weldon – the previous occupant – having been left on the rate book by mistake. Since the information in each rate book was copied from the one preceding it, the error was perpetuated for a number of years. It has been reported that Caroline Weldon was an aunt, though whether she was a blood relative or just a friend of the family it is not certain. The information comes from Langstaff,[15] who claims that it came from John Dickens' rent collector. The name of Caroline appears only once in the Dickens family tree, referring to Maria Caroline Barrow, an unmarried sister of Elizabeth Dickens.[16]

Two months after moving into Johnson Street John Dickens' retirement was imminent. A letter dated 28 February 1825 confirmed acceptance of Huskisson's recommendation:

Sir Having laid before the Lords Commissioners of His Majesty's Treasury your letter of the 14 Inst. inclosing copy of one from the Treasurer of the Navy recommending Mr. John Dickens a Clerk of the 3d Class in the Navy Pay Office for Superannuation; I am commanded by my Lords to acquaint you that under all the circumstances of this Case My Lords are pleased to concur with the Lords of the Admiralty in opinion that it will be proper to grant to Mr. Dickens a Retired Allowance of £145 per Annum[17]

John Dickens' final day of service with the Navy Pay Office was 9 March 1825 and his pension began on 10 March.[18] This, then, was the end of an era for John Dickens. During his twenty years with the Navy Pay Office he had grown from youth to manhood; had married and raised a family of seven children, of whom two had died; had toiled in Britain's two greatest naval dockyards and in the grand structure of Somerset House; had seen out two wars; had risen from a five-shilling-a-day 15th Assistant Clerk to a £350-a-year Clerk of the 3rd Class; had seen debt and imprisonment. A hard life, yet between the tears John Dickens can only be seen as cheerful and optimistic. And it is easy to imagine that he saw his retirement from the Navy Pay Office not as the end of an era, but as the beginning: there was a new home just on the edge of the countryside, a good pension, a legacy from his mother, a new career to look forward to, and he could once again consider further education for his eldest son: optimistic expansion shone brightly around the beginning of 1825!

RELEASE FROM WARREN'S

It is clear that throughout the time at Mrs Roylance's and Hampstead and into the Johnson Street period Charles was still, unhappily, working at Warren's. Conditions had been improved, however, by a removal of the business from Hungerford Stairs to Chandos Street in Covent Garden. Dickens wrote:

Next to the shop at the corner of Bedford-street in Chandos-street, are two rather old-fashioned houses and shops adjoining one another. They were one then, or thrown into one, for the blacking business; and had been a butter shop. Opposite to them was, and is, a public-house, where I got my ale, under these new circumstances. The stones in the street may be smoothed by my small feet going across to it at dinner-time, and back again. The establishment was larger now, and we had one or two new boys. Bob Fagin and I had attained to great dexterity in tying up the pots. I forget how many we could do, in five minutes. We worked, for the light's sake, near the

second window as you come from Bedford-street, and we were
so brisk at it, that the people used to stop and look in.
Sometimes there would be quite a little crowd there. I saw my
father coming in at the door one day when we were very busy,
and I wondered how he could bear it.

Now I generally had my dinner in the warehouse. Sometimes
I brought it from home, so I was better off. I see myself coming
across Russell-square from Somers-town, one morning, with
some cold hotch-potch in a small basin tied up in a handkerchief. I
had the same wandering about the streets as I used to have, and
was just as solitary and self-dependent as before; but I had not the
same difficulty in merely living. I never however heard one word
of being taken away, or of being otherwise than quite provided
for. At last, one day, my father, and the relative so often
mentioned, quarrelled; quarrelled by letter, for I took the letter
from my father to him which caused the explosion, but quarrelled
very fiercely. It was about me. It may have had some backward
reference, in part, for anything I know, to my employment at the
window. All I am certain of is, that, soon after I had given him the
letter, my cousin (he was a sort of cousin, by marriage) told me he
was very much insulted about me; and that it was impossible to
keep me, after that. I cried very much, partly because it was so
sudden, and partly because in his anger he was violent about my
father, though gentle to me. Thomas, the old soldier, comforted
me, and said he was sure it was for the best. With a relief so
strange that it was like oppression, I went home. My mother set
herself to accommodate the quarrel, and did so next day. She
brought home a request for me to return next morning, and a high
character of me, which I am sure I deserved. My father said, I
should go back no more, and should go to school. I do not write
resentfully or angrily: for I know all these things have worked
together to make me what I am; but I never afterwards forgot, I
never shall forget, I never can forget, that my mother was warm
for my being sent back.[19]

It is vitally important to note in this extract from Dickens'
fragment of autobiography that he writes of travelling into
Warren's from Somers Town, a clear indication of his continued
occupation at the blacking factory after having moved to Johnson
Street. This is of prime importance in assessing the length of time
that he worked at Warren's. He states himself of the length of this

period: 'I have no idea how long it lasted; whether for a year, or much more, or less.'[20] Past biographers have assumed that Dickens wildly miscalculated the length of the period: I suggest that he did not, and that it lasted until March or April 1825. The date he left Warren's must correspond closely with the date he commenced study at a new school, since Dickens himself wrote: 'My father said, I should go back no more, and should go to school.'[21]

Attempts to fix the date of his commencement at a new school have produced contradictory evidence, all coming from Dickens' schoolfriends. Forster confessed that he had heard very little from Dickens about the school,[22] but announced that he 'remained nearly two years, being a little over fourteen years of age when he quitted it'.[23] A schoolfellow, Owen P. Thomas, is reported to have put Dickens at the school for about two years, 1824–6,[24] and says that he entered a solicitor's office on leaving school.[25] Dr Henry Danson, another schoolfellow, also remembers Dickens being at the school for nearly two years, but says he was fifteen when he left,[26] which would shift the period to 1825–7. However, Langton reports that Dr Danson wrote to him that Dickens was there for two years, starting no later than June 1824 and leaving at Christmas 1825.[27] Langton also reports from another schoolfriend, John W. Bowden, that Dickens left in 1827.[28]

There seems general disagreement, then, upon the dates of Dickens' attendance at the school, though agreement on the period of two years. For reasons already stated he must have started some time after moving to Johnson Street, which was in the last week of 1824. I suggest that he began some time towards the end of March or at the beginning of April 1825, probably in the first week of the Midsummer Quarter, school fees, like so many other things, being paid by the quarter. This seems an appropriate time for the finances of John Dickens, since he retired from the Navy Pay Office on 9 March 1825 and thus made it possible to earn a salary in addition to his pension of £145 a year. It was more likely, therefore, that he could afford to do without Charles' small income and to pay the school fees. About two years from this date – which seems to be the period agreed among his schoolfellows as the length of Dickens' attendance – it is known that Dickens started work with the solicitor Molloy: in March 1827.

The revised length of Charles Dickens' employment at Warren's Blacking demands serious reassessment of this period of his life and the consequential reactions to it. To a twelve-year-old child a period of a year is an eternity; particularly if the end of that time cannot be seen, particularly if it is believed that there may be no end. Little surprise, then, that those twelve months were seared onto the mind of a child at such a formative age. It meant that the adult Dickens would carry that place with him in his head at all times, so that he continually made reference to it: in *Sketches by Boz* and *Pickwick*; in *Oliver Twist*, *Nicholas Nickleby* and the *Old Curiosity Shop*; in *David Copperfield*; in *Little Dorrit*, *Hard Times*, *Our Mutual Friend* and *Edwin Drood*.

It meant that the neglected or parentless child was a constant theme throughout his books: Oliver Twist, Little Nell, Smike, Paul Dombey, David Copperfield, Little Dorrit and Pip, for example. It meant that he always took a practical interest in the plight of poor and neglected young people, as with Urania Cottage. It meant that he forged a self-determination never again to be placed in such a detestable, powerless situation; a determination to succeed, always to have sufficient money, properly organised; a determination to be secure; and a determination that his own children should be happy, loved and comfortable.

It would be difficult to exaggerate the effect that Warren's Blacking had on the young Charles Dickens and consequently on his life and work. Biographers have recognised these effects, though have perhaps not quite understood why the period should have been so traumatic, believing it to have been only four to six months. It is more readily understood when that time is stretched to twelve or thirteen months.

WELLINGTON HOUSE ACADEMY

Dickens chose the end of his time at Warren's, and the recommencement of his education at Wellington House Academy, as the point at which to close his fragment of autobiography. He wrote:

> There was a school in the Hampstead-road kept by Mr. Jones, a Welshman, to which my father despatched me to ask for a card of terms. The boys were at dinner, and Mr. Jones was carving for them, with a pair of holland sleeves on, when I acquitted

myself of this commission. He came out, and gave me what I wanted; and hoped I should become a pupil. I did. At seven o'clock one morning, very soon afterwards, I went as day scholar to Mr. Jones's establishment, which was in Mornington-place, and had its school-room sliced away by the Birmingham-railway, when that change came about. The school-room however was not threatened by directors or civil engineers then, and there was a board over the door graced with the words WELLINGTON HOUSE ACADEMY.[29]

Here, then, was the achievement of something that Charles has passionately craved since arriving in London from Chatham. And yet we are not given the joy of this achievement in the same way that we are given the misery of its absence. Indeed the misery continued for a short while, as indicated by the parallel situation created in *David Copperfield*:

It seemed to me so long, however, since I had been among such boys, or among any companion of my own age . . . that I felt as strange as ever I had done in my life. I was so conscious of having passed through scenes of which they could have no knowledge, and of having acquired experience foreign to my age, appearance and condition as one of them, that I half believed it was an imposture to come there as an ordinary little schoolboy. I had become, in the Murdstone and Grinby time, however short or long it may have been, so unused to the sports and games of boys, that I knew I was awkward and inexperienced in the commonest things belonging to them. Whatever I had learnt, had so slipped away from me in the sordid cares of my life from day to night, that now, when I was examined about what I knew, I knew nothing, and was put into the lowest form of the school. But, troubled as I was, by my want of boyish skill, and of book-learning too, I was made infinitely more uncomfortable by the consideration, that, in what I did know, I was much farther removed from my companions than in what I did not. My mind ran upon what they would think, if they knew of my familiar acquaintance with the King's Bench Prison? Was there anything about me which would reveal my proceedings in connexion with the Micawber family – all those pawnings, and sellings, and suppers – in spite of myself? . . . What would they say, who

made so light of money, if they could know how I had scraped
my halfpence together, for the purchase of my daily saveloy
and beer, or my slices of pudding? How would it affect them, who
were so innocent of London life, and London streets, to discover
how knowing I was (and was ashamed to be) in some of the
meanest phases of both? All this ran in my head so much on that
first day . . ., that I felt distrustful of my slightest look and
gesture; shrunk within myself whensoever I was approached by
one of my new schoolfellows; and hurried off the minute school
was over, afraid of committing myself in my response to any
friendly notice or advance.[30]

I got a little the better of my uneasiness when I went to school
next day, and a good deal the better next day, and so shook it
off by degrees, that in less than a fortnight I was quite at home,
and happy, among my new companions. I was awkward
enough in their games, and backward enough in their studies;
but custom would improve me in the first respect, I hoped, and
hard work in the second. Accordingly, I went to work very
hard, both in play and in earnest, and gained great
commendation. And, in a very little while, the Murdstone and
Grinby life became so strange to me that I hardly believed in it,
while my present life grew so familiar, that I seemed to have
been leading it a long time.[31]

The misery of his non-school days remained bitter to Dickens
for a very long time, the misery compounded no doubt by his
lengthy period at Warren's. His bitterness was not, even in later
years with hindsight, allowed to be compromised by the sweetness
of his subsequent education. Indeed, during those later schooldays
the bitter past was not allowed to mix with the sweeter present,
nor would it ever be – a decision taken, it would seem, by the
family as a whole (though whether covertly agreed or overtly
understood it is impossible to say), since the period remained a
firm secret among Dickens' parents and his brothers and sisters;
even his own children knew very little of his childhood until after
his death. Dickens wrote in the fragment of autobiography: 'From
that hour until this, my father and my mother have been stricken
dumb upon it. I have never heard the least allusion to it, however
far off and remote, from either of them. I have never, until I now
impart it to this paper, in any burst of confidence with any one,

my own wife not excepted, raised the curtain I then dropped, thank God.'[32]

After he had written these words he read the account to his wife and gave the manuscript to his biographer, but shared his secret past with no other person throughout his life. Had he felt able to talk with close friends about his experiences it is possible that the resentment that he bottled up so tightly, and for so long, would not have exploded in such a way onto the pages of his fragment of autobiography and of *David Copperfield*. Within a year of the completion of *David Copperfield*[33] Dickens presented to the public another picture of his schooldays, this time hard but not so bitter – the bitterness having been purged, to some extent, by what he had already written. It was entitled 'Our School':

It was a school of some celebrity in its neighbourhood – nobody could have said why . . . The master was supposed among us to know nothing, and one of the ushers was supposed to know everything . . . The only branches of education with which he showed the least acquaintance, were ruling, and corporeally punishing. He was always ruling ciphering-books with a bloated mahogany ruler, or smiting the palms of offenders with the same diabolical instrument, or viciously drawing a pair of pantaloons tight with one of his large hands, and caning the wearer with the other. We have no doubt whatever that this occupation was the principal solace of his existence . . .

The usher at our school, who was considered to know everything as opposed to the Chief who was considered to know nothing, was a bony, gentle-faced, clerical-looking young man in rusty black . . . we all liked him; for he had a good knowledge of boys, and would have made it a much better school if he had had more power. He was writing-master, mathematical master, French master, made out the bills, mended the pens, and did all sorts of things . . . and he always called at Parents' houses to inquire after sick boys, because he had gentlemanly manners . . .

Our remembrance of Our School, presents the Latin master as a colorless doubled-up near sighted man with a crutch, who was always cold, and always putting onions into his ears for deafness, and always disclosing ends of flannel under all his garments, and almost always applying a ball of pocket-handkerchief to some part of his face with a screwing action round and round. He was a very good scholar, and took great pains when he saw intelligence and a desire to learn; otherwise, perhaps not . . .

There was a fat little dancing-master used to come in a gig, and taught the more advanced among us hornpipes (as an accomplishment in great social demand in after-life); and there was a brisk little French master who used to come in the sunniest weather, with a handless umbrella, and to whom the Chief was always polite, because (as we believed), if the Chief offended him, he would instantly address the Chief in French, and for ever confound him before the boys with his inability to understand or reply.

There was another school not far off, and of course our school could have nothing to say to that school. It is mostly the way with schools, whether of boys or men. Well! the railway has swallowed up ours, and the locomotives now run smoothly over its ashes.

So fades and languishes, grows dim and dies,
   All that this world is proud of,

– and is not proud of, too. It had little reason to be proud of Our School, and has done much better since in that way, and will do far better yet.[34]

Though Dickens was critical of the Wellington House Academy, he had earlier described it as a good school;[35] and though he entered it with burdens that he decided to carry alone, he nevertheless seemed to enjoy two years of typical schoolboy pursuits. A number of his schoolfriends later put their recollections on paper.[36] In them Dickens is described as a handsome, curly-headed lad, who held his head erect and was generally smartly turned out, usually wearing a jacket and trousers of a mixed black and white material. He was small but well-built, healthy-looking and full of energy and high spirits. His particular friends were Owen Thomas, Henry Danson, John Bowden and Daniel Tobin. Danson wrote:

At about that time Penny and Saturday Magazines were published weekly, and were greedily read by us. We kept bees, white mice, and other living things, clandestinely in our desks; and the mechanical arts were a good deal cultivated, in the shape of coach-building, and making pumps and boats, the motive power of which was the white mice.

I think at that time Dickens took to writing small tales, and we had a sort of club for lending and circulating them. Dickens was also very strong in using a sort of lingo, which made us quite unintelligible to bystanders. We were very strong, too, in theatricals. We mounted small theatres, and got up very gorgeous scenery to illustrate the *Miller and his men* and *Cherry and fair star*. Master Beverley constructed the mill for us in such a way that it could tumble to pieces with the assistance of crackers. At one representation the fireworks in the last scene, ending with the destruction of the mill, were so very real that the police interfered, and knocked violently at the doors. Dickens's after taste for theatricals might have had its origin in these small affairs.

I quite remember Dickens on one occasion heading us in Drummond-street in pretending to be poor boys, and asking the passers-by for charity – especially old ladies; one of whom told us she 'had no money for "beggar boys"'. On these adventures, when the old ladies were quite staggered by the impudence of the demand, Dickens would explode with laughter and take to his heels.[37]

Other contemporaries talk of the boys playing in Rhodes Fields behind Johnson Street, of a party at Johnson Street when Charles delivered with great energy and action the popular song 'The Cat's Meat Man', and of Charles distinguishing himself at school by taking the Latin prize – perhaps not surprisingly, bearing in mind that he had received the rudiments of Latin very early in life, from his mother in the Chatham days.[38] Close neighbours of the Dickenses were the Mitton family, who lived opposite, and Charles was particularly friendly with a daughter of the family, Mary Ann Mitton, who was his age. Another member of the family, Thomas Mitton, was to work with Dickens as a clerk a few years later and eventually worked as Dickens' solicitor for many years. Friends of Charles were later to describe Mrs Dickens as a delicate-looking woman and John Dickens as a father who took great interest in his son's progress.

Charles, it seems, took a similar interest in his father's progress, since he sought in a small way to emulate him. John Dickens had decided – and, with hindsight, quite rightly – that his future lay in journalism, and he had acquired a post with a well-established daily newspaper called *The British Press* (first published 1803). A colleague of John Dickens remembered Charles as 'a smart, intelligent, active lad, who brought what was then called, and is still, I believe, named, "penny-a-line staff"; – that is to say, notices of accidents, fires, police reports, such as escaped the more regular reporters, for which a penny a printed line was paid'.[39]

Exactly when and how John Dickens broke into journalism it is difficult to estimate (though his ability as a journalist had been demonstrated as early as 1820, when his account of the dreadful fire at Chatham had been published in *The Times* as well as the local paper). One biographer says he began with *The British Press* as early as January 1825,[40] although his work cannot be identified until September 1826. He may again have used the influence of his brother-in-law, John Henry Barrow, to obtain his post, since Barrow had been a contributor to that newspaper since 1822. John Dickens filled the position of a parliamentary correspondent, though he wrote a number of articles on marine insurance, these latter being signed 'Z'.[41] In these articles John Dickens showed particular support for the Lloyds insurance organisation, which subsequently awarded him a gift of ten guineas.[42] Apart from these articles it is difficult to identify John Dickens' other work, although it seems more than coincidence that his newspaper – carrying as it did extensive national and international news – should carry acounts of two meetings called to establish a road across Rhodes Fields, just behind the Dickens household.[43] It seems sensible that he should have commenced his career as a journalist immediately after retirement from the Navy Pay Office, but whether or not he cared to or was able to is a matter of conjecture.

As usual his financial arrangements were not well organised. £25 a year of his pension was being deducted at source to pay one of his creditors, John Dodd,[44] and the other debts he had incurred prior to his imprisonment were paid off in two payments, the first on 2 November 1825 and the second on 13 November 1826.[45] But Fanny's fees of 38 guineas a year at the Royal Academy of Music were not being paid properly. By 6 October 1825 a debt of £32 11s 11d was outstanding, and John Dickens sent an order for this amount to be deducted from his pension, but not until the end of the quarter 25 December! His accompanying letter read:

My dear Sir, Circumstances compel me to seek your friendly aid as on a former occasion by accepting in lieu of *present payment* an order as above. I flatter myself you will take some pleasure in forwarding my views in this respect with the Committee when I assure you that I shall consider it a most signal act of friendship. A circumstance of great moment to me will be decided in the ensuing term which I confidently hope will place me in comparative affluence, and by which I shall be enabled to redeem the order before the period of Christmas Day. At any rate it will meet with same attention as before, and I shall have the pleasure of expressing to you my sincere obligations.

I am looking forward with some hope . . .

And now, my dear Sir, it only remains for me to assure you of the sense I entertain of your general kindness and attention, and to subscribe myself, Your obliged and obedient servant, JOHN DICKENS.[46]

By the following Midsummer this amount had still not been paid, and a further sum had accrued, making a debt in all of £53 18s. In a letter to the committee in May 1826 John Dickens had asked to be allowed to pay off the debt at a rate of £10 quarterly, but £15 was asked for instead. This was obviously not adhered to, since a committee note dated 22 November 1826 stated that the money must be paid or Fanny withdrawn from the Academy. She left eight months later, in June 1827.[47]

And then came a further severe and unexpected blow to John Dickens: the collapse of *The British Press* at the end of October 1826. The increasing difficulties of his father heralded the completion of Charles Dickens' schooldays. And yet, almost like a sub-plot from one of Dickens' own later fictions, there were at this time of financial hardships promises of wealth to come, in the form of inheritances. First John Dickens' brother William died in December 1826, leaving to his wife, among other things, the interest on investments of £1000, but with the following clause:

Should my wife Sarah Dickens think proper to marry again at my decease she shall forfeit all claim to the interest of the £1,000 and that part of my will shall become null and void and in such case I request my friend Mr. Thomas Paul of Trevor Square,

Knightsbridge, gentleman, will carry out the latter part of my will and I give him £50 after he has proved such second marriage, paying out to Robert Street Chapel and fulfilling my last request, viz. that the remainder of the £1,000 go to surviving children of my brother John Dickens share and share alike.[48]

Speculation on the likelihood of getting the money and what might be done with it must have been rife.[49]

Then, on 12 June 1827, Richard Newnham, a good neighbour from their Chatham days with whom they had kept contact, died, leaving in his will a sixth share in the dividends of a £300 trust to Letitia. Later that year, in November, the last of the Dickens children was born and named Augustus Newnham Dickens (later nicknamed Moses, which was transformed to Bozes and finally commuted to Boz).

The uncertain financial position of the family came to a head, for Charles, in March 1827 when, at the age of fifteen, he was withdrawn from the Wellington House Academy. Some years later, in a letter to a publisher, he summarised the time concisely, and with a typically English style of understatement:

I had begun an irregular rambling education under a clergyman at Chatham, and I finished it at a good school in London – tolerably early, for my father was not a rich man, and I had to begin the world.[50]

Appendix: Street Plans

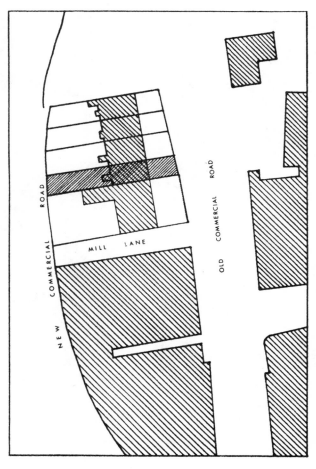

Charles Dickens' birthplace. (Michael Allen)

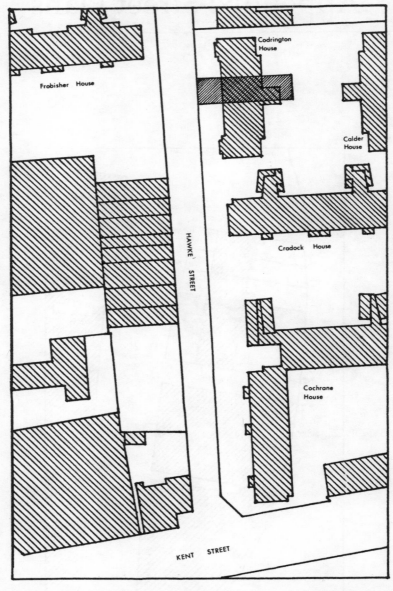

The Hawke Street area as it is now, showing the site of number 16. (Michael Allen)

The Wish Street area as it is now, showing the site of the house occupied by the Dickens family. (Michael Allen)

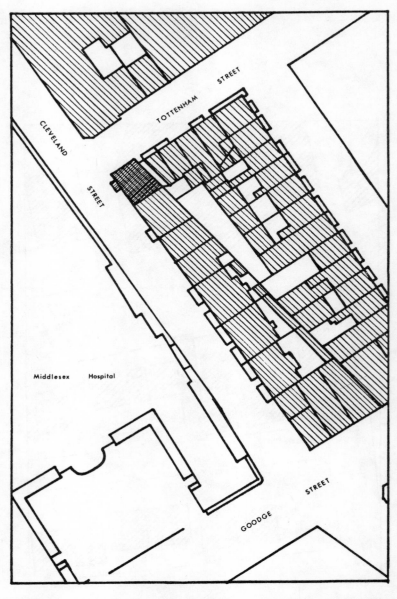

Cleveland Street as it is now, showing the site of what was 10 Norfolk Street.
(Michael Allen)

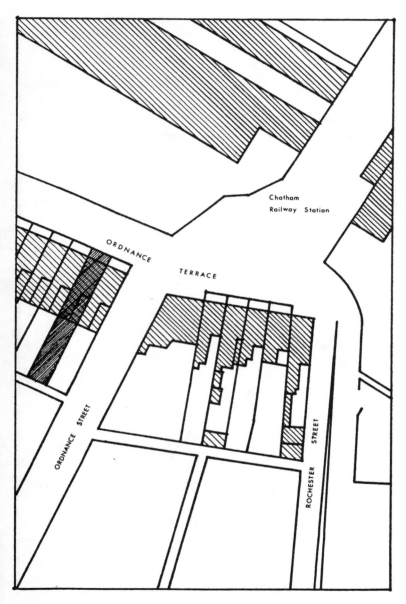

Site of 2 Ordnance Terrace. (Michael Allen)

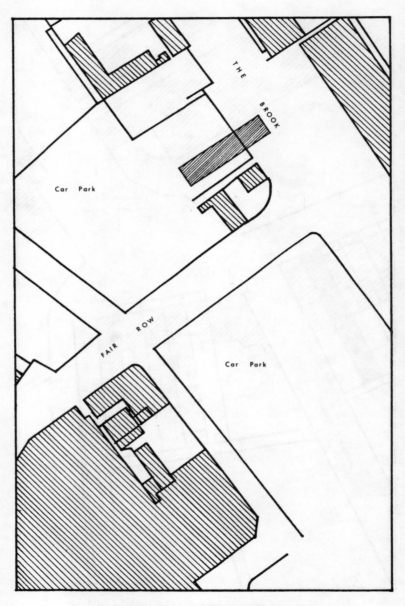

Site of 18 St Mary's Place, The Brook. (Michael Allen)

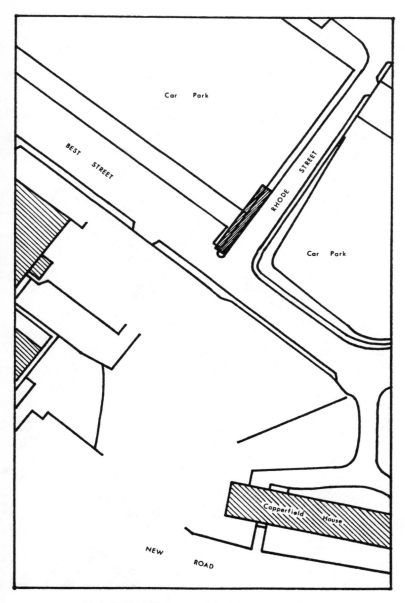

Site of Giles' House, Best Street. (Michael Allen)

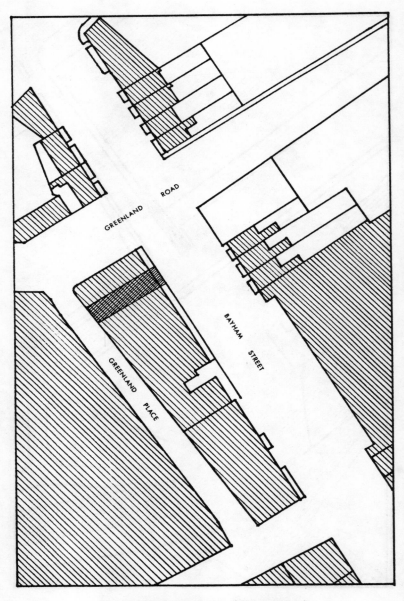

Site of 16 Bayham Street. (Michael Allen)

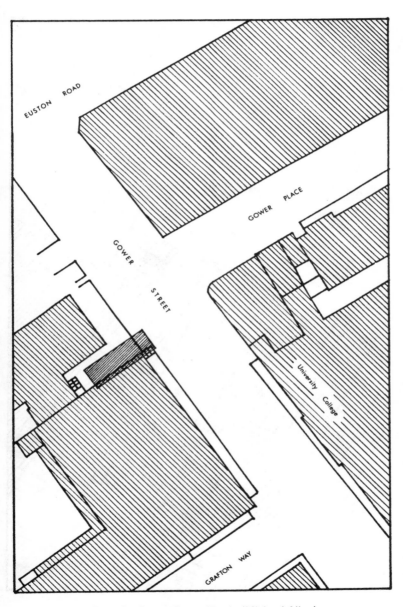

Site of 4 Gower Street North. (Michael Allen)

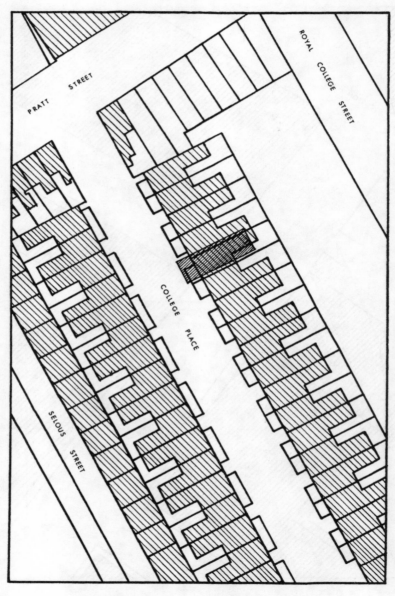

Site of 37 Little College Street. (Michael Allen)

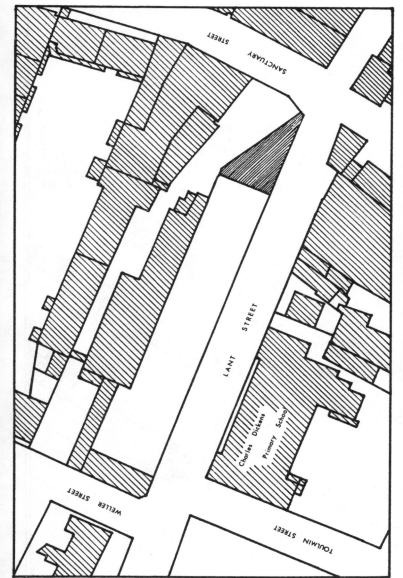

Site of 1 Lant Street. (Michael Allen)

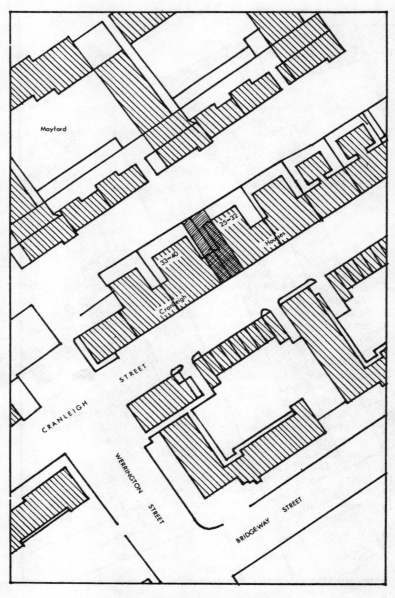

Site of 29 Johnson Street. (Michael Allen)

Notes

The place of publication is London unless otherwise stated.

INTRODUCTION

1. 'Dickens's obscure childhood in pre-Forster biography', by Elliot Engel, in *The Dickensian*, 1976, pp. 3–12.
2. *The letters of Charles Dickens*, Pilgrim edition, Vol. 1: 1820–1839 (Oxford: Oxford University Press, 1965) p. 423.
3. In *History*, xlvii, no. 159, pp. 42–5.
4. *The Pickwick Papers* (Harmondsworth: Penguin, 1972) p. 521.
5. John Forster, *The life of Charles Dickens* (Chapman & Hall, 1872–4) Vol. 3, p. 11.
6. Ibid., Vol. 1, p. 17.

1 PORTSMOUTH

1. Gladys Storey, *Dickens and daughter* (Muller, 1939) p. 31.
2, 'The Dickens ancestry: some new discoveries', in *The Dickensian*, 1949, pp. 64–73, 179–88.
3. Gladys Storey, op. cit., p. 32.
4. See Chapter 4, note 45.
5. 'The Dickens ancestry', op. cit.
6. T. Wemyss Reid, *The life, letters and friendships of Richard Monckton Milnes, first Lord Houghton* (Cassell, 1890) Vol. 2, p. 227.
7. As indicated in the Public Record Office papers (hereafter referred to as PRO), reference number ADM 7 819, p. 92.
8. PRO, ADM 7 3655.
9. One of the clerks was Charles Dilke, who many years later let slip to John Forster that he recollected the famous author spending part of his childhood working in a boot-blacking factory, unintentionally leading Dickens to write his fragment of autobiography.
10. PRO, ADM 22 11, p. 100.
11. PRO, ADM 22 11, p. 171; PRO, ADM 22 12, p. 7.
12. PRO, ADM 22 12, p. 49.
13. 'Leaves from my life', by Thomas Powell, in *Frank Leslie's Sunday Magazine*, Vol. xxi, February 1887, pp. 98–9.
14. PRO, ADM 49 72.
15. The first set of figures is taken from PRO, ADM 7 820, p. 281; the second set is compiled from a number of papers at the Public Record Office and differs in detail from a similar combination given by Angus Easson in *The Dickensian*, 1974, pp. 35–45.
16. PRO, ADM 1 3657, dated 6 December 1814.
17. PRO, ADM 49 72, dated February 1814.

18. Held at the Dickens Birthplace Museum.
19. *Hampshire Courier*, 1 June 1812.
20. It is reported that the parish authorities at St Mary's did not know they had the register of his baptism till after his death, when the executors wrote for it – Robert Langton, *The childhood and youth of Charles Dickens* (Hutchinson, 1891) p. 14.
21. Gladys Storey, op. cit., p. 25.
22. W. R. Hughes, *A week's tramp in Dickens-land* (Chapman & Hall, 1891) p. 285.
23. It appeared in the *Hampshire Telegraph and Sussex Chronicle* and the *Hampshire Courier*, both dated Monday 10 February 1812.
24. Forster, op. cit., Vol. 1, pp. 2–3.
25. Hughes, op. cit., p. 285.
26. Langton, *Childhood and youth*, op. cit., p. 17.
27. Hughes, op. cit., p. 285.
28. Frederic G. Kitton, *The Dickens country* (A. & C. Black, 1905) pp. 5–6.
29. James T. Fields, *Yesterdays with authors* (Boston: Houghton, Mifflin, 1887) pp. 233–4.
30. The announcement appeared in the *Hampshire Telegraph and Sussex Chronicle*, the *Hampshire Courier* and the *Hampshire Chronicle*, all dated Monday 4 April 1814.
31. *Hampshire Courier*, 10 January 1814.
32. Forster, op. cit., p. 2.
33. *Household Words*, 1 January 1859, Vol. 19, p. 98.
34. *Household Words*, 30 October 1852, Vol. 6, p. 146.
35. George Dolby, *Charles Dickens as I knew him* (Everett, 1912) pp. 37–8.
36. *Hampshire Courier*, *Hampshire Telegraph and Sussex Chronicle* and *Hampshire Chronicle*, all dated Monday 12 September 1814.
37. The register of burials in the Parish of Widley, held at the Portsmouth City Record Office.
38. Outport Allowance ceased to be paid to John Dickens from 1 January 1815 – PRO, ADM 22 14, p. 413.
39. That is, without payment of Outport Allowance, but with a rise in salary from £140 to £200 a year, due to him for ten years' service.

2 LONDON, 1815–16

1. PRO, ADM 22 14, p. 412.
2. Held at the Greater London Record Office.
3. 'The Dickens ancestry', op. cit.
4. Forster, op. cit., Vol. 1, p. 3.
5. See ' "The Deed" in David Copperfield', by W. J. Carlton, in *The Dickensian*, 1952, pp. 101–6.
6. See ' "I, Elizabeth Dickens": light on John Dickens's legacy', by Angus Easson, in *The Dickensian*, 1971, pp. 35–40.
7. *Household Words*, Christmas, 1855, p. 4.
8. *Household Words*, 1 January 1859, Vol. 19, p. 97.

3 SHEERNESS AND CHATHAM

1. *The Men of the time in 1852, or, Sketches of Living Notables* (David Bogue, 1852).
2. William Blanchard Jerrold, *The life and remains of Douglas Jerrold* (W. Kent, 1859) p. 10.
3. R. G. Hobbes, *Reminiscences and notes of seventy years' life, travel, and adventure*, 2 vols: *Vol. 2: Civil service in Sheerness and Chatham dockyards* (Elliot Stock, 1895). He was writing about a period some twenty years after John Dickens was there, but points out that little had changed over the years. Hobbes assisted Langton in his *Childhood and youth of Charles Dickens* and worked in the same office at Chatham as had John Dickens.
4. Ibid.
5. *David Copperfield* (Harmondsworth: Penguin, 1966) p. 238.
6. *The Pickwick Papers* (Harmondsworth: Penguin, 1972) p. 83.
7. Hobbes, op. cit., p. 103.
8. James Presnail, *Chatham: the story of a dockyard town and the birthplace of the British navy* (Corporation of Chatham, 1952) p. 194.
9. Information in this paragraph is taken form Presnail, op. cit., p. 103.
10. Ibid., pp. 230–2.
11. *Kentish Chronicle*, 1, 4 and 8 April 1817.
12. St Mary's Parish Records, Churchwardens Accounts, 1817–21, held at the Kent County Archives Office, ref. nos P85/5/43–46.
13. Langton, *Childhood and youth*, op. cit., p. 22.
14. Information on the baptisms is taken from the Register of Baptisms, St Mary's, Chatham, held at the Kent County Archives Office.
15. Langton, *Childhood and youth*, op. cit., p. 51.
16. Forster, op. cit., Vol. 1, p. 6.
17. Langton, *Childhood and youth*, op. cit., p. 26.
18. Forster, op. cit., Vol. 1, p. 6.
19. *Lippincott's Magazine*, Vol. xiii, June 1874, pp. 772–4.
20. Langton, *Childhood and youth*, op. cit., p. 26.
21. *Household Words*, 1 January 1859, Vol. 19, pp. 97–102.
22. Langton, *Childhood and youth*, op. cit., p. 22.
23. Ibid., p. 36.
24. Ibid., p. 35.
25. *Household Words*, Christmas 1855, p. 5.
26. Langton, *Childhood and youth*, op. cit., pp. 26–9.
27. The age of Mary Weller should be borne in mind here: she was born in 1804, so would have been only thirteen when the Dickens family arrived in Chatham and eighteen when they moved away.
28. *All the Year Round*, 8 September 1860, Vol. 3, pp. 517–21; reprinted as 'Nurses' stories' in *The Uncommercial Traveller* and in *Selected short fiction* (Harmondsworth: Penguin, 1976).
29. *All the Year Round*, 30 June 1860, Vol. 3, pp. 274–8; reprinted as 'Dullborough Town' in *The Uncommercial Traveller* and in *Selected short fiction* (Harmondsworth: Penguin, 1976).
30. *All the Year Round*, 8 September 1860, op. cit.

31. *Household Words*, 1 January 1859, op. cit.
32. *All the Year Round*, 30 June 1860, op. cit.
33. 'Some recollections of Dickens', by Marcus Stone, in *The Dickensian*, 1910, p. 63. The date was probably 2 November 1821, when the Prince Regent, recently made king, passed through on return from the continent – Frederick F. Smith, *A History of Rochester*. (C. W., Daniel & Co., 1928) p. 372.
34. *Household Words*, 15 May 1852, Vol. 5, pp. 189–92: 'First fruits', written with George Sala; reprinted in *The uncollected writings of Charles Dickens: Household Words 1850–1859*, edited by Harry Stone (Allen Lane, 1969). This latter book has notes and commentary on the article and reproduces pages from the book that Dickens quotes (pp. 409–19).
35. Langton, *Childhood and youth*, op. cit., p. 58.
36. *Household Words*, Christmas 1852; reprinted as 'The child's story' in *The Uncommercial Traveller*.
37. *All the Year Round*, 29 August 1863; reprinted as 'Chatham Dockyard' in *The Uncommercial Traveller*.
38. Langton, *Childhood and youth*, op. cit., p. 24.
39. *All the Year Round*, 6 June 1863, Vol. 9, pp. 348–52; reprinted as 'Birthday celebrations' in *The Uncommercial Traveller*.
40. Ibid.
41. Given in 'A Christmas tree' and 'Dullborough town', both in *Selected short fiction*, op. cit. See also Duane de Vries, *Dickens's apprentice years* (Hassocks, Sussex: Harvester Press, 1976).
42. *Household Words*, 15 May 1852, op. cit.
43. John Richardson was the Barnum of his day: at fairs throughout the country his players acted in booths scores of times daily. Richardson lived from 1760 to 1836.
44. A strangely derogatory description of the area in which he spent a happy childhood and for which he proved his affection later in life! – as was his later description of it as Dullborough Town.
45. Charles Dickens, *Memoirs of Joseph Grimaldi*, edited by Richard Findlater (Macgibbon & Kee, 1968) pp. 9–10. First published 1838.
46. Forster, op. cit., Vol. 1, p. 121.
47. Langton, *Childhood and youth*, op. cit., pp. 25–6.
48. *Household Words*, 11 October 1851: 'Our School'. This afterwards appeared in *Reprinted Pieces*.
49. *All the Year Round*, 30 June 1860, op. cit.
50. Langton, *Childhood and youth*, op. cit., pp. 23–4.
51. As shown in Presnail, op. cit., p. 201.
52. *The letters of Charles Dickens*, Pilgrim edition, op. cit., Vol. 1, p. 141.
53. For most of the information about the Newnhams see 'The old lady in Sketches by Boz', by William J. Carlton, in *The Dickensian*, 1953, pp. 149–52.
54. *Sketches by Boz* (Oxford: Oxford University Press, 1957).
55. *Lippincott's Magazine*, Vol. XIII, June 1874, pp. 772–4.
56. See 'John Dickens and the Navy Pay Office', by Angus Easson, in *The Dickensian*, 1974, pp. 35–45.

57. Hobbes, op. cit., p. 159.
58. Published in Rochester by W. Wildash, 1817.
59. William Jefferys, *An account of the dreadful fire at Chatham* . . . (Chatham: printed by C. and W. Townson, 1821).
60. First given by Langton, *Childhood and youth*, op. cit., p. 40.
61. His brother-in-law, John Henry Barrow, was at this time working for *The Times*.
62. William Jefferys, *An account of the dreadful fire at Chatham* . . ., op. cit.
63. '"The Deed" in David Copperfield', by W. J. Carlton, *The Dickensian*, 1952, p. 103.
64. Ibid.
65. *London Gazette*, 21 December 1824, p. 2140.
66. Forster, op. cit., Vol. 1, p. 3. Forster blunders badly by making no mention of Ordnance Terrace.
67. Given in F. G. Kitton's *The Dickens Country* (A. & C. Black, 1905) p. 14.
68. Forster, op. cit., Vol. 1, p. 8.
69. *Rochester & Chatham Journal*, 28 April 1888.
70. Gladys Storey, op. cit., p. 44.
71. *All the Year Round*, 6 June 1863, op. cit.
72. Langton, *Childhood and youth*, op. cit., p. 44.
73. *Household Words*, 1 January 1859, op. cit.
74. An account of William Giles is given in Arthur Humphreys, *Charles Dickens and his first schoolmaster* (Manchester: printed by Percy Brothers, 1926).
75. Langton, *Childhood and youth*, op. cit., pp. 56–63.
76. Humphreys, op. cit., p. 20.
77. *The speeches of Charles Dickens*, edited by K. J. Fielding (Oxford: Clarendon Press, 1960) pp. 50–1.
78. With reference to this description see Plate 20.
79. Forster got this address wrong – see Langton, op. cit., pp. 55–6.
80. Forster, op. cit., Vol. 1, p. 13.
81. Ibid., pp. 8–10.
82. See *Charles Dickens: an exhibition to commemorate the centenary of his death, June–September 1970* (Victoria & Albert Museum) p. 3; and Duane de Vries, op. cit., p. 6, note 19.
83. *The letters of Charles Dickens*, Pilgrim edition, Vol. 2: 1840–1841 (Oxford: Oxford University Press, 1969) pp. 267–8.
84. Langton, *Childhood and youth*, op. cit., p. 25.
85. Forster, op. cit., Vol. 1, p. 10.
86. She continued in Chatham until her death in 1888. An obituary notice appeared in the *Rochester and Chatham Journal* for 28 April 1888.
87. *All the Year Round*, Christmas 1859: 'The haunted house'; reprinted in *Christmas stories*. This line has been quoted by Forster, op. cit., Vol. 3, p. 218; by Langton, op. cit., p. 66; and by F. G. Kitton, *Charles Dickens: his life, writings and personality* (T. C. & E. C. Jack, 1902) p. 15.
88. Langton, *Childhood and youth*, op. cit., p. 63.
89. Forster, op. cit., Vol. 1, p. 15.
90. *All the Year Round*, 30 June 1860, op. cit.

91. Ibid.
92. Forster, op. cit., Vol. 1, p. 14.
93. *Household Words*, 1 January 1853, Vol. 6, pp. 361–3: 'Where we stopped growing'.
94. *Letters from Charles Dickens to Angela Burdett-Coutts, 1841–1865* (Cape, 1953) p. 315.
95. Forster, op. cit., Vol. ,1 p. 4.

4 LONDON, FROM CAMDEN TOWN TO THE MARSHALSEA

1. From a letter published in the *Daily Telegraph*, 7 December 1871.
2. St Pancras Poor Rate for the period 5 April 1822 to 29 September 1822; rate made 16 July 1822. Held at Holborn Public Library, London Borough of Camden.
3. Kitton, *Charles Dickens: his life, writings and personality*, op. cit.
4. Forster, op. cit., Vol. 1, p. 18.
5. Ibid., p. 16.
6. Ibid., p. 42.
7. *Sketches by Boz*: 'The streets – morning'.
8. *Sketches by Boz*: 'Seven Dials'.
9. Forster, op. cit., Vol. 1, p. 19.
10. *Household Words*, 13 August 1853, Vol. 7, pp. 553–7: 'Gone astray'.
11. MS letter in Robert Langton's *Childhood and youth of Charles Dickens*; held at the British Library, ref. DEX c61.b.15.
12. 'The barber of Dean Street', by W. J. Carlton, in *The Dickensian*, 1952, pp. 8–12.
13. Forster, op. cit., Vol. 1, p. 22.
14. St Pancras rate books: 17 of the 45 houses in Bayham Street received summonses for this period.
15. 'Fanny Dickens, pianist and vocalist', by W. J. Carlton, in *The Dickensian*, 1957, pp. 133–43.
16. A note is made in the lighting and watching rate book for Gower Street North, for the half year ending 29 September 1823, to the effect that Mrs Dickens commences Xmas, at number 4. An extensive search has failed to uncover an illustration or photograph of this house.
17. Kitton, *The Dickens country*, op. cit., p. 27.
18. Forster, op. cit., Vol. 1, p. 24.
19. Ibid.
20. *David Copperfield*, op. cit., pp. 213–14.
21. *Early Victorian England, 1830–1865* (Oxford: Oxford University Press, 1934) Vol. 1, p. 45.
22. Gladys Storey, op. cit., p. 52.
23. Edgar Johnson, *Charles Dickens: his tragedy and his triumph* (Gollancz, 1953) p. 34.
24. Michael Slater, *Dickens and women* (Dent, 1983) pp. 156–7.

25. Forster, op. cit., Vol. 1, pp. 31–3.
26. He was admitted to the Marshalsea Prison on 20 February 1824 (PRO, Prisons 11/7, Commitment Book).
27. Forster, op. cit., Vol. 1, p. 23.
28. Ibid., p. 24.
29. *David Copperfield*, op. cit., p. 222.
30. In a letter to John Forster from the husband of the granddaughter, Mr P. Wood. The letter is held in the Forster Collection at the Victoria & Albert Museum, London (ref. FD.18.33) and is mentioned by W. J. Carlton in his 'Postscripts to Forster', in *The Dickensian*, 1962, p. 88.
31. Forster, op. cit., Vol. 1, pp. 35–7.
32. *The Pickwick Papers*, op. cit., p. 376.
33. Forster, op. cit., Vol. 1, pp. 37–8.
34. Ibid., pp. 38–9.
35. For example, *Bowles's one-sheet plan of the Cities of London and Westminster with the Borough of Southwark*, 1801.
36. *Pigot's London & Provincial New Commercial Directory, 1822–1828.*
37. Poor rate books for St George the Martyr, Southwark, North Division; held at the John Harvard Library, London Borough of Southwark.
38. He is listed in *Clarke's New Law List for 1824*, where he is also noted as a Vestry-Clerk for St George's, Southwark.
39. In *Pigot & Co's National, London & Provincial Commercial Directory for 1832–3–4* (J. Pigot) p. 599.
40. Forster, op. cit., Vol. 1, p. 40.
41. *The Pickwick Papers*, op. cit., p. 521.
42. Forster, op. cit., Vol. 1, p. 39.
43. PRO, ADM 1 3659.
44. Ibid.
45. This is the only reference I have been able to find to John Dickens' age. If he was in his 39th year at the time the letter was written, then he must have achieved 39 some time between April 1824 and March 1826, and was therefore born between April 1785 and March 1786. His father, it may be recalled, died in October 1785.
46. PRO, ADM 1 3659.
47. Given in the death certificate, held at the General Register Office, and reported in Angus Easson's 'John Dickens and the Navy Pay Office', op. cit., p. 41.
48. Forster, op. cit., Vol. 1, pp. 44–6.
49. In a letter to Thomas Beard, given in Angus Easson's 'John Dickens and the Navy Pay Office', op. cit. Also in a letter to his wife, dated 25 March 1851: 'My dearest Kate, I have been greatly hurried and shocked today. Mr. Davey came here this morning, to say that he thought it impossible my father could live many hours. He was in that state from active disease (of the bladder) which he had mentioned to nobody, that mortification and delirium terminating in speedy death, seemed unavoidable. Mr. Wade was called in, who instantly performed (without chloroform) the most terrible operation known in surgery, as the only chance of saving him. He bore it with astonishing

fortitude, and I saw him directly afterwards – his room, a slaughter house of blood. He was wonderfully cheerful and strong-hearted. The danger is that the wounds will slough and he will fall into a low fever – but the strength of his constitution may save him. I have been about, to get what is necessary for him, and write with such a shaking hand that I cannot write plainly.' – from *Mr. & Mrs. Charles Dickens: his letters to her*, edited by Walter Dexter (Constable, 1935) pp. 150–1.

50. Forster, op. cit., Vol. 1, p. 42.
51. Taken from Angus Easson's ' "I, Elizabeth Dickens": light on John Dickens's legacy', in *The Dickensian*, 1971, pp. 35–40. The will is preserved in the Greater London Record Office (DL/C/487).
52. *David Copperfield*, op. cit., pp. 223–4.

5 RELEASE FROM PRISON, RELEASE FROM WARREN'S, AND BACK TO SCHOOL

1. Forster, op. cit., Vol. 1, p. 46.
2. *David Copperfield*, op. cit., p. 231.
3. Forster, op. cit., Vol. 1, p. 69.
4. *The letters of Charles Dickens*, Pilgrim edition, op. cit., Vol. 1, p. 47.
5. Ibid., p. 6.
6. PRO, ADM 1 3659.
7. First mentioned by Forster, op. cit., Vol. 1, p. 46, as 'a small house in Somers Town', and p. 26 as 'a very small house in a street leading out of Seymour-street'.
8. John Brett Langstaff, *David Copperfield's library* (Allen & Unwin, 1924) p. 61.
9. William Hone, *Year book of daily recreation and information* . . . (Tegg, 1832) p. 318.
10. These were discovered under five or six layers of wallpaper – Langstaff, op. cit., p. 68.
11. Information taken from Langstaff, op. cit., p. 61.
12. Kitton, *Charles Dickens: his life, writings, and personality*, op. cit., p. 19.
13. Poor rate books for the Parish of St Pancras. Held at the Holborn Branch Library of the London Borough of Camden.
14. The number was changed from 29 to 13 at Christmas 1825.
15. Langstaff, op. cit., p. 51.
16. 'The Dickens ancestry', op. cit.
17. PRO, ADM 1 3659.
18. Dates supplied by two items in Public Record Office: ADM 1 3660, dated 28 February and 3 March 1828, and Pension Books, PRO, PMG 24/1–4 – given by Angus Easson, 'John Dickens and the Navy Pay Office', op. cit.
19. Forster, op. cit., Vol. 1, pp. 47–9.
20. Ibid., p. 49.
21. Ibid.

22. Ibid., p. 65.
23. Ibid., p. 54.
24. Ibid., p. 56.
25. Ibid., p. 60.
26. Ibid., p. 61.
27. Langton, *Childhood and youth*, op. cit., p. 85.
28. Ibid., p. 88.
29. Forster, op. cit., Vol. 1, p. 54.
30. *David Copperfield*, op. cit., pp. 284–5.
31. Ibid., p. 293.
32. Forster, op. cit., Vol. 1, p. 49. See also 'Dickens's past: some facts and surmises', by Stanley Tick, in *The Dickensian*, Spring 1982, pp. 29–41.
33. The autobiographical statement was probably written in 1847, *David Copperfield* between 1849 and 1850, and the following article, 'Our School', in 1851.
34. *Household Words*, 11 October 1851, op. cit.
35. In a letter written in 1838 – see *The Letters of Charles Dickens*, Pilgrim edition, op. cit., Vol. 1, p. 423.
36. Owen Thomas and Henry Danson in Forster; these two and John Bowden in Langton; R. Shiers in the *Camden Gazette*, 16/12/1871; and an unnamed schoolfriend in *The Dickensian*, 1911, pp. 229–31.
37. Forster, op. cit., Vol. 1, pp. 62–3.
38. The Latin tutor was Richard Shiers, who was later presented with a book by Dickens as a token of gratitude – see Thomas Wright's *The Life of Charles Dickens* (Jenkins, 1935) p. 45.
39. Samuel Carter Hall, *Retrospect of a long life, from 1815 to 1883* (Bentley, 1883) Vol. 1, p. 111.
40. Una Pope-Hennessy, *Charles Dickens, 1812–1870* (Chatto & Windus, 1945) p. 12.
41. See W. J. Carlton's article 'John Dickens, journalist', in *The Dickensian*, 1957, pp. 5–11.
42. *The Dickensian*, 1928, p. 175.
43. *The British Press*, 13 and 21 October 1826.
44. Angus Easson, 'John Dickens and the Navy Pay Office', op. cit.
45. *London Gazette*, 22 October 1825; and 27 October 1826, announcing 'a second and final dividend' – reported by Easson, in *The Dickensian*, 1971, p. 40.
46. Reprinted in *The Dickensian*. 1913, p. 148.
47. Carlton, 'Fanny Dickens, pianist and vocalist', op. cit.
48. 'The Dickens ancestry', op. cit.
49. It came to them in September 1836.
50. *The letters of Charles Dickens*, Pilgrim edition, op. cit., Vol. 1, p. 423.

Bibliography

This bibliography lists all works referred to in the text, plus a number of other titles that were consulted in the course of writing this book. The place of publication for each item is London, unless stated otherwise.

Adrian, A. A., *Georgina Hogarth and the Dickens circle* (Oxford: Oxford University Press, 1957).

All the Year Round, Christmas 1859.
—— Vol. 3, 30 June 1860.
—— Vol. 3, 8 September 1860.
—— Vol. 9, 6 June 1863.
—— Vol. 10, 29 August 1863.

Allbut, Robert, *London rambles 'en zigzag' with Dickens* (Edward Curtice, [1886]).

Allbut, Robert, *Rambles in Dickens-land* (Chapman & Hall, 1903).

Balfour, Alan, *Portsmouth (City Buildings Series)* (Studio Vista, 1970).

Bowen, W. H., *Charles Dickens and his family: a sympathetic study* (Cambridge: W. Heffer (privately printed), 1956).

Bowles's one-sheet plan of the Cities of London and Westminster with the Borough of Southwark, 1801.

The British Press, 13 and 21 October 1826.

Brown, Ivor, *Dickens in his time* (Nelson, 1963).

Camden Town Gazette, 16 December 1871.

Camden Town Poor Rate Books, 1822–4.

Camden Town rate books for watching, lighting, watering, cleansing, gravelling and otherwise improving the foot carriage, 1822.

Carlton, William J., 'The barber of Dean Street', in *The Dickensian*, 1952.

Carlton, William J., ' "The Deed" in David Copperfield', in *The Dickensian*, 1952.

Carlton, William J., 'In the blacking warehouse', in *The Dickensian*, 1964.

Carlton, William J., 'Fanny Dickens, pianist and vocalist', in *The Dickensian*, 1957.

Carlton, William J., 'John Dickens, Journalist', in *The Dickensian*, 1957.

Carlton, William J., 'The old lady in Sketches by Boz', in *The Dickensian*, 1953.

Carlton, William J., 'Postscripts to Forster', in *The Dickensian*, 1962.

Chancellor, E. Beresford, *The London of Charles Dickens* (Richards, 1924).

Chancellor, E. Beresford, *London's old Latin quarter, being an account of Tottenham Court Road and its immediate surroundings* (Cape, 1930).

Chatham gaol rate books, 1816–20.

Chatham St Mary's parish records: churchwarden's accounts, 1816–23.

Chatham St Mary's parish records: register of baptisms, 1819–20.

Clarke's new law list for 1824.

Daily Telegraph, 7 December 1871.

Davey, E., 'The parents of Charles Dickens': a letter to the editor, in *Lippincott's Magazine of popular literature and science*, Vol. XIII, June 1874.

Dawson, Robert K., *Plans of the cities and boroughs of England and Wales*, 2 vols (printed by James and Luke G. Hansard & Sons, 1832).

De Vries, Duane, *Dickens's apprentice years* (Hassocks, Sussex: Harvester Press, 1976).

Dickens, Charles, 'Birthday celebrations', in *All the Year Round*, Vol. 9, 6 June 1863.

Dickens, Charles, 'Chatham dockyard', in *All the Year Round*, Vol. 10, 29 August 1863.

Dickens, Charles, 'The child's story', in *Household Words*, Christmas 1852.

Dickens, Charles, 'A christmas tree', in *Household Words*, Vol. 2, 21 December 1850.

Dickens, Charles, *David Copperfield* (Harmondsworth: Penguin, 1966).

Dickens, Charles, 'Dullborough Town', in *All the Year Round*, Vol. 3, 30 June 1860.

Dickens, Charles, 'First fruits', in *Household Words*, Vol. 5, 15 May 1852.

Dickens, Charles, 'Gone astray', in *Household Words*, Vol. 7, 13 August 1853.

Dickens, Charles, 'The haunted house', in *All the Year Round*, Christmas 1859.

Dickens, Charles, 'The Holly-tree Inn', in *Household Words*, Christmas 1855.

Dickens, Charles [Letters], *Dickens to his oldest friend. The letters of a lifetime from Charles Dickens to Thomas Beard*, edited by Walter Dexter (Putnam, 1932).

Dickens, Charles [Letters], *Letters from Charles Dickens to Angela Burdett-Coutts, 1841–1865* (Cape, 1953).

Dickens, Charles [Letters], *The letters of Charles Dickens*, Pilgrim edition, Vol. 1: 1820–1839, edited by Madeline House and Graham Storey (Oxford: Oxford University Press, 1965).

Dickens, Charles [Letters], *The letters of Charles Dickens*, Pilgrim edition, Vol. 2: 1840–1841, edited by Madeline House and Graham Storey; associate editor Kathleen Tillotson (Oxford: Oxford University Press/Clarendon Press, 1969).

Dickens, Charles [Letters], *Mr. & Mrs. Charles Dickens: his letters to her*, edited by Walter Dexter (Constable, 1935).

Dickens, Charles, 'Lying awake', in *Household Words*, Vol. 6, 30 October 1852.

Dickens, Charles, *Memoirs of Joseph Grimaldi*, edited by Richard Findlater (MacGibbon & Kee, 1968).

Dickens, Charles, 'New Year's Day', in *Household Words*, Vol. 19, 1 January 1859.

Dickens, Charles, 'Nurses' stories', in *All the Year Round*, Vol. 3, 8 September 1860.

Dickens, Charles, 'Our school', in *Household Words*, Vol. 4, 11 October 1851.

Dickens, Charles, *The Pickwick Papers* (Harmondsworth: Penguin, 1972).

Dickens, Charles, *Selected short fiction* (Harmondsworth: Penguin, 1976).

Dickens, Charles, *Sketches by Boz* (Oxford: Oxford University Press, 1957).

Dickens, Charles, *The speeches of Charles Dickens*, edited by K. J. Fielding (Oxford: Clarendon Press, 1960).

Dickens, Charles, *The uncollected writings of Charles Dickens: Household Words, 1850–1859*, edited by Harry Stone (Allen Lane 1969).

Dickens, Charles, *The uncommercial traveller, and Reprinted Pieces* (Oxford: Oxford University Press, 1958).

Dickens, Charles, 'Where we stopped growing', in *Household Words*, Vol. 6, 1 January 1853.

'The Dickens ancestry: some new discoveries', in *The Dickensian*, 1949.

The Dickensian, 1905–84.

Dolby, George, *Charles Dickens as I knew him* (Everett, 1912).

Dunn, Frank T., *A cumulative analytical index to The Dickensian 1905–1974* (Hassocks, Sussex: The Harvester Press, 1975).

Early Victorian England, 1830–1865 (Oxford: Oxford University Press, 1934) Vol. 1.

Easson, Angus, ' "I, Elizabeth Dickens": light on John Dickens's legacy' in *The Dickensian*. 1971.

Easson, Angus, 'John Dickens and the Navy Pay Office', in *The Dickensian*, 1974.

Easson, Angus, 'The mythic sorrows of Charles Dickens', in *Literature and History*, No. 1, March 1975.

Engel, Elliot, 'Dickens's obscure childhood in pre-Forster biography', in *The Dickensian*, 1976.

Fields, James T., *Yesterdays with authors* (Boston: Houghton Mifflin, 1887).

Forster, John, *The Life of Charles Dickens* (Chapman & Hall, 1872–4) 3 vols.

Francis, David, *Portsmouth old and new* (E.P. Publishing, 1975).

Frank Leslie's Sunday Magazine, Vol. xxi, February 1887.

Goss, Charles W. F., *The London directories, 1677–1855: a bibliography with notes on their origin and development* (Denis Archer, 1932).

Greaves, John, 'I was born on a Friday', in *A guide to the Charles Dickens Birthplace Museum* (1970).

Hall, Samuel Carter, *Retrospect of a long life: from 1815 to 1883* (Bentley, 1883) 2 vols.

Hampshire Chronicle, 4 April and 12 September 1814.

Hampshire Courier, 5 November 1810.

—— 10 February and 1 June 1812.

—— 20 December 1813.

—— 4 April, 12 September and 26 December 1814.

Hampshire Telegraph and Sussex Chronicle, May 1808.

—— 5 November 1810.

—— 20 and 27 January 1812.

—— 10 February and 7 March 1812.

—— 4 April and 12 September 1814.

Harvey, John H., *Sources for the history of houses* (British Records Association, 1974).

Hibbert, Christopher, *The making of Charles Dickens* (Longman, 1967).

Higham, Charles, *The adventures of Conan Doyle* (Hamish Hamilton, 1976).

History, xlvii, no. 159.

The history and antiquities of Rochester and its environs (Rochester: W. Wildash, 1817).

Hobbes, R. G., *Reminiscences and notes of seventy years' life, travel, and adventure*, 2 vols: *Vol. 2: Civil Service in Sheerness and Chatham dockyards* (Elliot Stock, 1895).

Hone, William, *The year book of daily recreation and information . . .* (Tegg, 1832).

Horwood, Richard, *Plan of the cities of London and Westminster and the Borough of Southwark, and parts adjoining shewing every house* (1792–9).

Household Words, Vol. 4, 11 October 1851.

—— Vol. 5, 15 May 1852.

—— Christmas 1852.

—— Vol. 6, 1 January 1853.

—— Vol. 6, 30 October 1852.

—— Vol. 7, 13 August 1853.

—— Christmas 1855.

—— Vol. 19, 1 January 1859.

Howarth, A. J., 'Dickens birthplace museum', in *A guide to the Charles Dickens Birthplace Museum* (1970).

Hughes, W. R., *A week's tramp in Dickens-land* (Chapman & Hall, 1891).

Humphreys, Arthur, *Charles Dickens and his first schoolmaster* (Manchester: printed by Percy Brothers, 1926).

Ireland, Samuel W. H., *A new and complete history of the county of Kent* (G. Virtue, 1828–30) 4 vols.

Jefferys, William, *An account of the dreadful fire at Chatham, which happened on Friday the 3rd of March, 1820 . . .* (Chatham: printed by C. and W. Townson, 1821).

Jerrold, William Blanchard, *The life and remains of Douglas Jerrold* (W. Kent, 1859).

Johnson, Edgar, *Charles Dickens: his tragedy and triumph* (Gollancz, 1953).

Johnstone's London commercial guide and street directory, 1818–30.

Kentish Chronicle, 1, 4 and 8 April 1817.

Kitton, F. G., *Charles Dickens: his life, writings and personality* (T. C. & E. C. Jack, 1902).

Kitton, F. G., *Charles Dickens by pen and pencil* (1890).

Kitton, F. G., *The Dickens country* (A. & C. Black, 1905).

Korg, J. (editor), *London in Dickens's day: a book of primary source materials* (Prentice Hall, 1961).

Langstaff, John Brett, *David Copperfield's library* (Allen & Unwin, 1924).

Langton, Robert, *Charles Dickens and Rochester* (Chapman & Hall, 1880).

Langton, Robert, *The childhood and youth of Charles Dickens* (Hutchinson, 1912).

Lippincott's Magazine of Popular Literature and Science, 'The parents of Charles Dickens', a letter to the editor from E. Davey (Philadelphia: Lippincott, 1874).

List of books, prints, portraits, autograph letters & memorials exhibited at Dickens' Birthplace Museum, 393 Commercial Road, Portsmouth, compiled by Alfred A. Seale (Portsmouth: W. H. Barrell, 1914).

Lloyd, David W., *Buildings of Portsmouth and its environs: a survey of the dockyard, defences, homes, churches, commercial, civic and public buildings* (Portsmouth: City of Portsmouth, 1974).

London Gazette, 21 December 1824.

—— 22 October 1825.

—— 27 October 1826.

Mackenzie, Norman and Jeanne, *Dickens: a life* (Oxford: Oxford University Press, 1979).

The men of the time in 1852, or, sketches of living notables (David Bogue, 1852).

Miller, Frederick, *Saint Pancras: past and present* (Heywood, 1874).

Norton, Jane E., *Guide to the national and provincial directories of England and Wales, excluding London, published before 1856* (Royal Historical Society, 1950).

Notes and Queries, to 1947.

Oliver, John, *Dickens' Rochester* (Rochester: Hallewell Publications, 1978).

Palmer, Samuel, *St. Pancras: being antiquarian, topographical, and biographical memoranda* (Palmer, 1870).

The picturesque beauties of Great Britain; illustrated by topographical, historical, and critical notices; combining every interesting object, ancient and modern: Kent (George Virtue, [c. 1830]).

Pigot & Co's National, London & Provincial Commercial Directory for 1832–3–4.

Pigot's London & Provincial New Commercial Directory, 1822–1828.

Pope-Hennessy, Una, *Charles Dickens, 1812–1870* (Chatto & Windus, 1945).

Portsmouth City Museum, *A guide to the Charles Dickens Birthplace Museum* (Portsmouth: City Museum Publications, 1970).

Portsmouth gaol rate books, 1809–14.

Portsmouth register of baptisms in the Parish of Portsea, 1810–14.

Portsmouth register of burials in the Parish of Widley, 1814.

Post-office annual directory, 1806 and 1815–30.

Powell, Thomas, 'Leaves from my life', in *Frank Leslie's Sunday Magazine*, vol. xxi, February 1887.

Presnail, James, *Chatham: the story of a dockyard town and the birthplace of the British navy* (Corporation of Chatham, 1952).

'Recollections of Charles Dickens, by a school-fellow and friend', in *The Dickensian*, 1911.

Reeve, Lovell Augustus, *Photographic portraits of men of eminence in literature, science, and art, with biographical memoirs*, no. xxxi, January 1866 (Lovell Reeve & Co., 1867).

Reid, T. Wemyss, *The life, letters and friendships of Richard Monckton Milnes, first Lord Houghton* (Cassell, 1890) 2 vols.

Richardson, A. E., 'No. 13 Johnson Street, Somers Town', in *Not so bad as we seem* (published for the Children's Libraries Movement by the Rolls Publishing Co., 1921).

Riley, R. C., *The growth of Southsea as a naval satellite and Victorian resort* (Portsmouth: City Council, 1972).

Robson's improved London directory, street guide and carrier's list, 1820, 1822 and 1826.

Rochester and Chatham Journal, 28 April 1888.

St George the Martyr, Southwark, poor rate books (North Division), 1824.

St Marylebone rate books, 1815 and 1816.

St Marylebone register of baptisms for 1816.

St Pancras lighting and watching rate book, 1822–4.

St Pancras poor rate books, 1821–2.

St Pancras watering rate book, 1824.

Saunders, Mrs Baillie, *The great folk of old Marylebone* (n.d.).

Sherry, J. Ashby, 'Charles Dickens in Southwark', in *English Illustrated Magazine*, November 1888.

Slater, Michael, *Dickens and women* (Dent, 1983).

Smith, F. Hopkinson, *In Dickens's London* (New York: Scribner, 1914).

Smith, Frederick Francis, *A history of Rochester* (C. W. Daniel & Co., 1928).

Staples, Leslie, 'Two early London homes of Charles Dickens', in *The Dickensian*, 1951.

Stephens, W. B., *Sources for English local history* (Manchester: Manchester University Press, 1973).

Stone, Marcus, 'Some recollections of Dickens', in *The Dickensian*, 1910.

Storey, Gladys, *Dickens and daughter* (Muller, 1939).

Storey, Richard, and Lionel Madden, *Primary sources for Victorian studies: a guide to the location and use of unpublished materials* (Phillimore, 1977).

Taylor, Theodore, *Charles Dickens: the story of his life, by the author of the 'Life of Thackeray'* (Hotten: second edition, 1871). Sometimes given as written by H. T. Taverner and J. C. Hotten.

Tick, Stanley, 'Dickens's past: some facts and surmises', in *The Dickensian*, 1982.

Victoria & Albert Museum, *Charles Dickens: an exhibition to commemorate the centenary of his death, June–September 1970* (1970).

Ward, H. Snowden and Catherine, W. B., *The real Dickens land* (Chapman & Hall, 1904).

Wright, Thomas, *The life of Charles Dickens* (Jenkins, 1935).

Index

References to Dickens' works are listed under title.
References to Dickens' characters are listed under the work in which they appear.